D1553059

Child Custody

Child Custody

A Study of Families after Divorce

Deborah Anna Luepnitz
Philadelphia Child
Guidance Clinic

LexingtonBooks
D.C. Heath and Company
Lexington, Massachusetts
Toronto

Library of Congress Cataloging in Publication Data

Luepnitz, Deborah Anna.
  Child custody.

  Includes bibliographical references and index.
  1. Children of divorced parents—United States. 2. Custody of children
—United States. 3. Family—United States. 4. Divorce—United States.
I. Title.
HQ777.5.L83   306.8'7   80-8787
ISBN 0-669-04365-6   AACR2

Published simultaneously in Canada

Printed in the United States of America

International Standard Book Number: 0-669-04365-6

Library of Congress Catalog Card Number: 80-8787

*This book is dedicated to my mother and father,
and to Jorge Rogachevsky.*

Contents

List of Figure and Tables   xi

Preface and Acknowledgments   xiii

Chapter 1   Introduction   1

                 The Law   2
                 Social-Science Views of Divorce and Custody   4
                 Maternal, Paternal, and Joint Custody   8
                 Questions Addressed by This Investigation   13
                 Author's Theoretical Perspective   14
                 Theory of Investigation   16
                 Limitations of the Study   17
                 Overview of Study Procedures and Quantitative
                     Findings   17

Chapter 2   The Custody and Visitation Arrangements   23

                 How the Mothers Attained Custody   23
                 How the Fathers Attained Custody   24
                 Who Helped in Making the Custody Decision   26
                 Consulting Children about Custody   26
                 Parents' Satisfaction with Custody   28
                 Anxiety over Losing Custody   31
                 Children's Satisfaction with Custody   32
                 Visitation   33
                 The Joint-Custody Family   37
                 The Problematic Joint-Custody Families   48
                 Conclusions   52

Chapter 3   Economics   55

                 Income Data   55
                 Alimony and Child Support   57
                 Work   59
                 Managing Money   61
                 Moving   62
                 Credit   64
                 Economic Advantages of Single Parenthood   65

Economics and the Joint-Custody Families   67
Conclusion: The Economics of Divorced
    Motherhood   72

Chapter 4   **Authority**   75

Locus of Responsibility: Single-Custody Parents   76
Changes in Style   77
Are Two Authorities Better than One?   82
Children's Role in Changing the Authority
    Structure   85
Advantages to Disciplining as a Single Parent   89
Joint-Custody Families   90
Conclusions   96

Chapter 5   **Domestics**   99

Change in Amount of Housework Performed   99
Coping   103
Advantages   105
Joint Custody and Domestics   106
Conclusions: Solo Parenting in the Space Age   108

Chapter 6   **Child Care**   111

Becoming the Primary Caretaker   111
Substitute Care   112
Contact and Closeness with Children   116
The Cost of Closeness   119
Conclusions   120

Chapter 7   **Support Systems**   123

Loneliness: Single-Custody Mothers and Fathers   123
The Support Group   124
Social Stigma   132
Children's Support Systems   135
Joint Custody   140
Conclusions   145

Chapter 8   **Conclusions**   149

Children's Adjustment in the Three Custody
    Types   149
Joint Custody: The Answer?   150

	Many Kinds of Families	152
	Future Investigation	155
	Why It Is Important that Men Mother	155
	Families of the Future	157
Appendix A	**The Sample**	161
Appendix B	**Statistical Results**	165
Appendix C	**Research Instruments**	169
	References	183
	Index	189
	About the Author	192

List of Figure
and Tables

Figure

8-1   Pros and Cons for Parents of Each Custody Type   151

Tables

2-1   Percentage of Maternal and Paternal Children in Five
      Visitation Patterns   34

3-1   Median Income for Men and Women before and after
      Divorce   56

3-2   Parents' Ratings of How Much They Worry about
      Money   56

3-3   Financial Arrangements of the Joint Families   67

4-1   Who Disciplines?   76

6-1   Percentage of Children in Each Custody Type who
      Have Experienced Substitute Care   113

6-2   Percentage of Parents Using More Substitute Care after
      Divorce than before   115

7-1   Percentage of Parents Who Felt There Was Overlap
      between Their Pre- and Postdivorce Support Groups   124

7-2   Percentage of Parents Whose Relatives Provide
      Supportive "Services"   127

7-3   Percentage of Parents Who Date Regularly   129

7-4   Percentage of Parents Who Desired to Remarry   131

7-5   Percentage of Parents Who Felt that Single Parenthood
      Enhanced or Diminished Their Social Status   133

Preface and Acknowledgments

This book was written primarily for a professional audience—for researchers, therapists, lawyers, and judges who are interested in the postdivorce family. It is not a manual to help parents, nor is it a treatment guide for therapists. Its purpose simply is to place questions about child custody in a historical and intellectual context and to begin to answer those questions with information gathered from interviews with fifty families practicing maternal, paternal, or joint custody.

The families were recruited in Buffalo, New York, and in Cleveland, Ohio, in 1978. All names have been changed for reasons of confidentiality.

The epigraph is reprinted from Toni Morrison's *Song of Solomon* (copyright, 1977) with kind permission from Alfred A. Knopf, Inc.

Acknowledgments

The anthropologist Miguel Barnet has said that an investigation is not successful if, at the time you say good-bye, there is not sadness on both sides. Although our relationship was brief, I felt connected with each of the fifty families, and I thank them deeply for allowing me to enter their homes at odd hours to answer my odd questions.

It is a pleasure also to thank three people who, at distant points en route to this book, mothered my thoughts. They are Donald Vicarel, Claire Schneider, and Larry Andrews.

This book is a revision of my doctoral dissertation. I am grateful for the patience and help of my committee: Steven Tulkin, Barbara Bunker, and Nancy Johnson. Norman Rosenberg, the outside reader, is the person who first pointed out to me the need for research on custody. He has been more than generous with his talent during the past five years.

Murray Levine chaired the dissertation and acted as my major advisor throughout graduate school. Without him I could not have undertaken a dissertation that departed so greatly from the reductionist traditions of academic psychology. More than that, Murray has been a role model embodying Rodin's exhortation *"toujours travailler."* He is the most productive man I have ever met, and he has *never* been too busy for me.

During the year the manuscript was in preparation, I was an intern at the Philadelphia Child Guidance Clinic. I am indebted to Dr. Marla Isaacs of the Families of Divorce Project who allowed me to present my ideas at her team meetings and who taught me a great deal about divorce and about therapy.

I would like especially to thank Sally Robinson because this book bears the mark of her deft mind, and because her friendship has been inspiration and solace.

For their kindness and support, I thank: Herbert Blumberg, Jane Archer, Diane Warden, Patricia Landman, George Saba, Karlotta Bartholomew, and Ann Itzkowitz.

Without a doubt, I have learned more about families from my own family—both immediate and extended—than from any other source. I am profoundly grateful to Doris, Gerard, and Rebecca Luepnitz, who taught me how to love and how to fight.

Finally, Jorge Rogachevsky has read and criticized and consoled and Xeroxed for the sake of this project, and loved its author more than anyone. ". . . *el poeta eres tú.*"

This research was funded partially by the Danforth Foundation, which sustained me financially throughout graduate school.

They say she screamed and screamed, lost her mind completely. You don't hear about women like that anymore, but there used to be more—the kind of woman who couldn't live without a particular man. And when the man left, they lost their minds, or died or something. Love, I guess. But I always thought it was trying to take care of children by themselves, you know what I mean? —Toni Morrison, *Song of Solomon*

1 Introduction

Two historical developments in the life of the American family form the ground for this inquiry. The first is the rise in the rate of divorce in the past two decades, and the second is the change in the social organization of gender stimulated by the feminist movement.

The divorce rate jumped 125 percent between 1960 and 1976[1]. If this trend continues, one-third of all children born in 1990 will spend part of their childhood in a single-parent family (Glick 1979). Nearly all these children would have lived with their mothers after the divorce, dining out with their fathers on Sunday, were it not for the second set of changes—those in sex-role norms. The simplest way of summarizing this complex set of changes is to say that in the past two decades, women have become increasingly involved in the *public sphere* (that is, the world of production) and men have become more involved in the *private sphere* (that is, the world of reproduction). Talcott Parsons' definition of the healthy family as having a male parent who specializes in "instrumental" tasks (for example, doing, earning money) and a female parent specializing in "expressive" tasks (for example, feeling, caring for children) does not fit the family of 1980.

Economic factors, of course, have contributed substantially to the influx of women into the labor force. Economics, however, cannot explain the interest many men have shown in parenting and, in general, in discovering their affective selves. The following advice on fathering from Bruno Bettelheim in 1956 now sounds quaint even to the lay ear:

> The male physiology . . . is not geared to infant care. . . .The relationship between father and child never was and cannot now be built principally around child-care experiences. It is built around a man's function in society: moral, economic, political.[2]

A quick perusal of the child-care shelf of a typical bookstore now reveals such titles as *How to Father,*[3] *Father and Child*[4] and *Who Will Raise the Children?*[5] Popular culture offers us heroes such as Ted Kramer[6] and Garp[7], whose lives are unquestionably child centered. Even the opinion of some experts has changed. Benjamin Spock, whose best-selling baby book once warned women against involving men in daily baby care, now maintains that such involvement is desirable and "natural."[8]

One result of the nascent change in the social organization of gender is that men have become increasingly vocal about their treatment as the "disposable parent'' after divorce.[9] Men have begun to organize groups (for example, ''Fathers For Equal Rights'') to help each other fight for custody. As of 1974 there were over 800,000 children living alone with their fathers.

Some mental-health professionals are enthusiastic about the increased interest in paternal and joint custody. Others, however, view as pernicious anything different from what is often referred to as ''traditional mother custody.'' This phrase is something of an oxymoron since mother custody has a relatively short history in the law. Before proceeding to social-scientific evidence pro and contra men's ability to parent, the history of child-custody law will be briefly reviewed.

The Law

Before 1900, Anglo-American law encountered little controversy with regard to custody (Foster 1973). The father had a property interest in his children, and woman was almost a legal nonentity. Mothers hardly seemed the more appropriate guardians of children since women themselves were thought of as requiring protection. Not only would a woman need to prove her husband's unfitness but she would also have to be wealthy enough to support her child since respectable women did not work. An interesting historical footnote is that the first man in England ever to lose custody of his children was the poet Percy Shelly, whose atheism and romantic adventures shocked the court and induced it to grant custody to Mary Shelly. (Mary too was later deprived of custody because of her activism in the contraception movement.) By the turn of the century, women had begun to receive custody of children in many cases. The switch from father to mother is attributable to at least three historical factors: (1) the firm entrenchment of the Industrial Revolution, which divided the (male) world of wage labor from the (female) domestic world; (2) the changing concept of childhood, away from the Victorian notion that children need discipline and moral guidance above all to the modern notion that children need love and nurturance above all; and (3) the political victories for women resulting from the early feminist movement.

This switch from father to mother custody was initiated into judicial writing through the ''tender-years'' doctrine. As early as 1839, a U.S. judge wrote that despite man's traditional right to custody, the child in question would be placed with the mother because of the child's ''tender age'' that is, twenty-one months.[10] In that case the court pronounced that nature had given women a unique attachment to children and that the baby would thus receive better care from its mother. The exact definition of tender years was determined by each judge. In the case referred to, the child was returned to her father at age four; that is when she was deemed old enough to separate from her mother. In later years judges used age seven for the upper limit of tender years. In practice, tender years was simply extended to include all minors.

In 1925 Judge Cardozo introduced into his opinion the phrase "best interests of the child" as the criterion for placement.[11] He shifted the focus away from the desires of the embattled parents in order to protect the child by acting as *parens patriae*. At the present time, the phrase "best interests of the child" has been included in the statutes of all but two states.

Judge Cardozo's ruling obviously did not remove the difficulty of defining the best interests of a given child in a particular situation. Weiss (1978) has pointed out that the language of custody law is so vague that judges often base decisions on their personal beliefs about motherhood, fatherhood, and what the American family should be like. Because most judges are elderly, white men, their opinions are often criticized for being relentlessly conventional.

From the 1920s until the 1960s, the best interests of children were defined as maternal custody. The reason for judges' inclination toward or "presumption for" mothers must be sought outside legal doctrine. One interpretation is that the notion of a "maternal instinct," which underlies the courts' presumption, was invented to keep women at home, "in their place." When women are needed in the labor force, as they were during World War II, less is said about maternal instinct.[12]

Many contemporary authors have denounced the court's presumption for mothers as anachronistic and sexist. There are others, however, who argue for preserving maternal presumption. Presumption does cut down on the number of disputed custody cases that place heavy demands on the courts and on the families involved. Presumption is also used to protect both women accused of adultery and lesbian mothers. That is, if the court believes fervently enough in the child's need for his or her mother, it may overlook the issue of the mother's sexual activity.

Not until the late 1960s did the controversy over women's and men's rights to parent re-ignite. Fifteen states now have statutes affirming the rights of women and men to be judged equally as potential custodians. In practice, however, judicial opinion has just begun to reflect a trend away from maternal presumption. The 1938 pronouncement that "there is but a twilight zone between a mother's love and the atmosphere of heaven"[13] still looms large in the courtroom.

An alternative aimed at solving the dilemma of choosing between parents is *joint custody*. Joint custody has many definitions, and is sometimes used interchangeably with "shared custody," "cocustody" and "coparenting." In this book *joint custody* will refer to that arrangement in which parents share equally the responsibility for making vital decisions about the child. The child's physical care and residence may or may not be shared equally between the parents.

Joint custody is not popular with judges. Petitions for a joint award have been rejected on the grounds that it would be injurious to the child. One judge has stated:

> It has been written on the pages of all times that no man can serve two masters, and it is certainly true that no child can pursue a normal life when subjected to the precepts, example and control of first one person and then another.[14]

In a recent opinion denying a petition for joint custody, the judge wrote, "Divorce dissolves the family as well as the marriage—a fact that may not be ignored."[15]

Despite judicial resistance, eleven states now have laws authorizing joint custody, and several states are now considering bills that would require judges to begin with a presumption for the joint award. In 1980 California signed into law Assembly Bill 1480, which is very favorable to the joint award. The statute was designed to create an expectation that "joint physical and legal custody will prevail unless it can be proved by a parent that sole custody is in the best interests of the child."[16] There is another provision in the statute reminiscent of King Solomon's judicial wisdom. If the California court should decide that sole custody is best in a given case, it is required to consider, among other things, "which parent is more likely to allow the child . . . frequent and continuing contact with both parents. . . ."[17]

One point on which everyone agrees is that decisions on child custody are among the most difficult that judges face. Many lawyers and judges have sounded a plea to psychologists for immediate research attention to the issue of custody. What data *can* social science offer at the present time, regarding the effects on children of maternal, paternal, and joint custody? A review of the literature follows.

Social-Science Views of Divorce and Custody

Research of the 1950s and 1960s

Lindsy Van Gelder in a recent article captured the image of children of divorce of the 1950s:

> When I was growing up in the Eisenhower swamplands, children whose parents underwent divorce were said to be "products of a broken home." The phrase was invariably uttered in a pitying stage whisper, and for me it conjured up drastic images of flotsam, jetsam and kamikaze fighter planes slicing through the roofs of suburban split-levels.[18]

If social science of this period did not create the myth of divorce as disaster, it did not do much to evaluate it. There are no studies of the 1950s that actually included comparisons of the lives of two-parent and single-parent families. Research on divorce instead focused on the highly specific "impacts" of "broken homes" on their "victims." There exists today an enormous "father-absence" literature, in which the attempt is made to link this lone variable with a host of life problems such as delinquency, underachievement, promiscuity, and confused sexual identity. In 1973 Herzog and Sudia reviewed this literature. They examined over two hundred studies dealing with the consequences of father absence. They concluded that while many studies *did* report negative effects in father-absent versus father-present children, many other studies found no such effects, and a few found positive effects associated with father absence. Herzog and Sudia concluded that other factors in the lives of children (for example, their socioeconomic status, characteristics of the mother, and the presence of other adults) overshadowed the effects of father absence *per se.*

Five years later Mary Beth Shinn reviewed the father-absence literature. She found sixteen sound studies that linked poor cognitive development with father absence. Twelve studies, on the other hand, found either no effects or positive effects associated with father absence. In contrast with Herzog and Sudia, Shinn concluded that father absence *is* a predictor of poor cognitive performance. Shinn herself noted, however, that even in the studies labeled as methodologically sound, the socioeconomic controls were "rough." In some cases, the absent father's occupation was the sole indicator of the single mother's socioeconomic status. This is indeed a rough indicator since the income of divorced mothers is only 53 percent of the couple's previous joint income (Glick 1979).

Nearly all commentators agree that father absence *is* related to poverty and that poverty is related to a variety of psychosocial problems. Thus Herzog and Sudia concluded that the father-absence studies could show us only something that was already well established, that is, that poor children fare less well than richer children.

While sympathetic to the position of Herzog and Sudia, I do not wish to trivialize the significance of family structure for the developing child. Certainly, a child who grows up with mother alone will face different problems from those of the child who grows up with father alone, or the child who grows up with two parents, or the child raised in a commune. Personality is formed in the family. It would be as unreasonable to suppose that father absence makes no difference as it would be to conclude that it causes delinquency. The question has not been posed in the most useful way. The father-absence studies follow what has been described as the "billiard-ball" model of research in which one examines the impact of one discrete event on another discrete event. Those correlational studies have revealed very little about what it means for an individual to grow up with or without a father. They have revealed nothing at all, of course, about what it means for the fathers themselves or the single mothers. The father-absence studies historically seem to fulfill the Parsonian dictum that healthy families have a division of labor whereby women are "expressive" and men are "instrumental." Given this theoretical model, it is logical to predict that children growing up without a man in their home to model success, achievement, and intellect will grow up delinquent, underachieving, and less intelligent.

Studies of the 1970s and 1980s

Recent studies of divorce have exhibited more sophistication in their attempt to understand the complexity of family life. The most famous of these studies is that of Judith Wallerstein and Joan Kelly, which they report in *Surviving The Break-Up*.[19] Wallerstein and Kelly studied sixty familiies (including 131 children) from the time of the separation through a five-year follow-up. One of their goals was to generate normative data on the responses of children to divorce. The authors are quite correct in asserting that their project has no peer in the United States or in Europe. The study's scope is most impressive: every child of each family, along with both custodial and noncustodial parents, was studied. Teachers also were interviewed about children's progress. The study included not one but two follow-ups—eighteen months and five years after the separation.

The authors discovered that the child's developmental level was the best predictor of its particular response to the divorce. For example, preschool children responded to the separation by regressing in their toilet-training or speech. They were confused about the meaning of the separation and often blamed themselves for it. Latency children, on the other hand, seemed depressed and angry about the break-up.

At the eighteen-month follow-up, nearly half the children were still symptomatic, and some were actually worse than at the initial interview. Even at the five-year follow-up, 37 percent were "moderately to severely depressed." The authors found serious acting out in many of the adolescents, and children of all ages still wished their parents would reconcile.

The position of Wallerstein and Kelly is obviously that divorce is an egregious experience for children. Nonetheless, the authors do not ignore the issues of coping and mastery. They acknowledge, for example, that there were adolescents in their sample who exhibited insight and compassion unusual in individuals who have not undergone a crisis like divorce. They also report a finding that is quite interesting in light of the preoccupation of the father-absence literature with cognitive deficits: overall, the school performance of the children in the sample did not suffer. The performance of some improved, and that of others declined, but there was no general negative trend as earlier theorists would have predicted.

It is important to note that the sample described in *Surviving The Break-Up* is almost certainly skewed toward the most distressed end of the divorced population. The researchers solicited participants by promising counseling over a five-year period, which no doubt attracted a sample distressed enough to want help.

Wallerstein and Kelly found several factors to be associated with positive outcome. The two most important seem to be: (1) easy access to the noncustodial parent and (2) a postdivorce mother-father relationship that is relatively conflict free.

These results are corroborated in the work of Mavis Hetherington and her colleagues at the University of Virginia. Hetherington et al. studied ninety-six preschool children, half of whom had divorced parents. The authors found that one year after the separation, children of divorced parents were functioning more poorly than control children in a number of ways. First, they were "less affectionate" with their parents, and "less obedient" to their commands. Second, children from divorced homes were rated more negatively by both their peers and their teachers.[20] As the authors pointed out, this disturbance cannot be linked causally with the divorce. Years of living in an unhappy home could have interfered with their social development. In any case, all the children of divorce had improved by the two-year follow-up. The sexes did not improve to the same degree, however. On nearly all measures of children's behavior, the girls from divorced homes were functioning much better than the boys from divorced homes. It is interesting that Wallerstein and Kelly found a similar sex difference at the first follow-up. It is possible that mothers are better able to relate to their daughters than to their sons after divorce. This important issue will be addressed later.

For many students of the family, the main question unanswered by studies like those just reviewed is, would it be better for children if the parents had stayed together? No one would disagree that an intact but unhappy family is not the healthiest environment for children. Can we conclude that such a home is more debilitating than a happy one-parent home?

Michael Rutter's (1971) study produced compelling results with regard to this question. He found three times more delinquency among children of divorce than among children whose father had died. If father-absence were the key variable, then there should have been no difference between these groups. Rutter concluded that it was the domestic turbulence that precedes divorce, and that usually does not precede death, that was key. Several recent studies (for example, Hess and Camara 1979) have found that parental conflict is a better predictor of children's maladjustment than is the

marital status of the parents (that is, divorced or married). Raschke and
Raschke (1979) studied 280 grade-school children and found that the self-
concept scores of children were significantly lower in families where parental conflict was high. Self-concept, however, was independent of whether
the family type was intact, single-parent, or reconstituted.

The studies of family conflict are impressive but are called into question
by the demographic studies that have found an overrepresentation of
children of divorce among clinic populations (for example, Mc Dermott
1970; Tuckman 1966; Kalter 1977). If parental discord were the more
critical stressor, we would expect our clinics to be overrepresented by
children of married, embattled parents.

Is it better for children to grow up with two parents who are in conflict
or in a postdivorce family that is conflict free? My own early work emphasized the dangers of domestic turmoil (Luepnitz 1978, 1979), but this
emphasis seems now like oversimplification. Robert Weiss once quipped
wisely at a conference, "To ask whether divorce is good or bad is neither an
interesting nor an important question. The question is, how does it work?"

This book concerns itself not with the good and bad of divorce but with
how it works—more specifically with how three custody alternatives work.
We turn now to examine the existing literature on paternal and joint
custody.

Maternal, Paternal, and Joint Custody

The literature on child custody cannot compare with the literature on
divorce and children in quantity or quality. The reason is simple: Trends
in nonmaternal care are so recent that there have not been enough fathers
or joint custodians to study. Even at this time it is very difficult to collect
a sample that is demographically representative. This study, for all its
limitations, is the first to compare families in all three custody situations.
We turn now to review the existing literature on fathering and joint
custody.

Can Men Mother?

Nearly everyone agrees that, throughout the ages, whether or not it has been
necessary, women have raised the children. In all the societies we know
of—industrial and nonindustrial, pre- and postrevolutionary—women have
had the primary responsibility for child care. The fact that women are
anatomically equipped for *childbearing* does not explain why they have also
had the task of caring for children who are weaned.

There have been several attempts to explain female-dominated child care. One is that a woman's biological makeup creates not only the capacity for childbirth but also qualities of personality such as empathy. Alice Rossi, for example, contends that if men were to be primary caretakers of infants, they would require special training to make up for their lack of female hormones.[21]

The notion that biology alone accounts for women's history as primary caretakers was challenged by Harlow et al. in their 1970 experiments. They found that monkeys who grew up alone were unable to care for their own offspring. These animals, whose "instincts" were presumably intact, had been deprived of the benefit of social learning and thus did not know how to care for their babies.

There is an anthropological theory about mothering that holds that women have always raised the children not because they were driven by instinct but because childbirth and lactation made it impossible for them to do anything else. Indeed, in early societies women were pregnant most of the time, due to the absence of contraceptive devices. Many births were required, moreover, to ensure species survival since infant mortality was extremely high.

This argument may in fact be valid for *hunting* societies. It would have been inexpedient and dangerous for pregnant women to chase and kill large game. Pregnancy, however, has not prevented women in other kinds of societies from doing hard work. In agricultural societies, women have worked the fields with babies strapped to their backs and hips.[22] Certainly, in modern times there is no biological reason why one sex should care for the children while the other works in an office. Nonetheless, it continues to be the case—even in our relatively progressive nation, and even in contemporary Cuba and Sweden where women's equality is protected by law—that not only are women responsible for most of the home childcare, but they also constitute nearly 100 percent of all daycare workers.

The other major explanation for female-dominated childcare is the role-training argument. In other words, women mother because as girls they were pressured to play with "girl" toys and were rewarded for being gentle and soft whereas boys were made to play with "boy" toys and were rewarded for being aggressive and tough. Maccoby and Jacklin (1974) report fascinating research that shows the many and subtle ways in which parents and teachers prepare boys for achievement and girls for motherhood. This social pressure is maintained by other institutions, as well as by the mental-health establishment, as the classic study by Broverman et al. illustrated.[23]

Role-training theory has made a great contribution to our understanding of gender and has understandably dominated academic psychology. Psychoanalytic theory, however, which is not incompatible with learning theory, states that gender identity is achieved through a process more subtle and profound than social coercion. The analytic argument is that gender is formed not only through the *content* of what parents expect from boys and girls but also by the *structure* of the parent-child relationships from birth onward. A new contribution to the psychoanalytic argument is Nancy Choderow's powerful book, *The Reproduction of Mothering*. Choderow criticizes both the biological and the social-learning theories of mothering and emphasizes the relationship between the infant and its first perceived "other." The fact that in every case—in all societies we know of—the first "other" is a woman, is of profound significance. It creates an assymetry that is the beginning of the difference between male and female psychology. Choderow contends that mothers experience a primary sameness with their infant girls and a primary "differentness" from their infant boys. Girls, nurtured by a same-sex parent, grow up with a sense of self as continuous with their first "other." Boys, nurtured by an opposite-sex parent, experience themselves as discontinuous with their first "other." Girls thus develop an ego that is predicated on *relatedness* to their emotional context and boys on *separateness* from theirs. The sex-role indoctrination that children later receive is thus an extension of the subtle psychological processes (largely unconscious) that have already occurred as a result of a family structure in which women mother. Choderow concludes that changing the social organization of gender will involve more than changing children's toys and textbooks. It is a much larger task than most social scientists imagine but nonetheless a change that Choderow sees as very desirable. If children were dependent from birth on people of both sexes, they would not develop "fears of *maternal* omnipotence and expectations of *women's* unique self-sacrificing qualities."[24] This, she believes,

> would reduce men's needs to guard their masculinity and their control of social and cultural spheres . . . and would help women to develop the autonomy which too much embeddedness in relationship has often taken from them.[25]

The question that Choderow does not directly confront is whether or not a man raised in the traditional family structure (that is, by an opposite-sex parent) *can* mother as well as a woman, and if so, what in her theory would explain this capacity.

No one has studied the family-of-origin experience of men who become active parents. The only study that speaks at all to this issue was done by Kelin Gersick in 1979. Gersick was interested in why some men chose to seek custody of their young children after divorce while other men did not. He found that men who sought custody described themselves as closer to their mothers than to their fathers and were more likely to have an older brother and a sister. He speculated that a child who follows both male and female siblings may be less bound by gender norms since the parents would have already focused their anxiety about creating sex-appropriateness in the older siblings.

Until recently, little thought has been given to developing men's potential for childcare. Some fascinating work done recently on fathers and infants has shown that infants show no preference for either parent in their display of attachment behavior (Lamb 1977). Most of the research on fathering, however, has dealt not with infants but with school-aged children being raised by their fathers after divorce. The best of these studies is reported in *Fathers Without Partners,* by Rosenthal and Keshet (1981). The authors studied 127 fathers with varying degrees of contact with their children after divorce. All fathers said that fathering had led to their own personal growth, as it required them to develop their empathy and emotional responsiveness, and to be less compulsive about their careers. Rosenthal and Keshet maintain that adults need children just as children need adults to be complete individuals. Unfortunately, their interviews included fathers only. Children were not interviewed nor was any direct assessment made of father-child interaction.

Santrock and Warshak (1979), on the other hand, did a study including both fathers and children after divorce. Their sample of sixty families consisted of one-third with mother custody, one-third with father custody, and one-third intact families. For our purposes, the most important of their comparisons were between children in father custody and mother custody. One clear result emerged: Children living with the same-sex parent were more socially competent than those living with the cross-sex parent. Boys living with fathers were more "mature," "social," and "independent" than girls living with their fathers. Conversely, girls living with mothers were more competent than boys living with mothers. Recall that in Hetherington's study of mother custody, the boys functioned more poorly than the girls.

Santrock and Warshak suggest that parents may simply find it easier to identify with same-sex children and therefore to become closer with them. In some cases, the cross-sex child may remind the custodial parent of the ex-spouse, and hostility may be transferred to the child. All clinicians have probably heard a divorced parent lamenting, "This child is the spitting image of my ex-spouse, and I'm afraid I see the same personality developing."

This fascinating set of issues and speculations about same-sex and cross-sex parenting is the most recent contribution of the divorce literature. All of this work, as well as Choderow's book, postdates the data-collection phase of this study. Thus the parents in this sample unfortunately were not asked about differences in the relationships with their sons and daughters. This is a rich area for future investigation.

Joint Custody

Despite the absence of research on custody, strong opinions have formed pro and contra the joint award. The most disparaging view of shared custody is offered by Goldstein, Freud, and Solnit in *Beyond the Best Interests of the Child*. The authors posit that because of children's need for "unbroken continuity" of affectionate relationships with "an adult," courts should make custody determinations with utmost dispatch. Drawn-out custody battles—wherein children's placement is indefinite for a period of time—are to be avoided at all costs. They point out that the child's sense of time is different from that of adults; that is, one month to a seven-year-old can seem an eternity. The authors contend further that the psychological tie between a parent and a young child can be severed by even a brief separation.

Much more controversial than the preceding statements is the authors' emphasis on establishing one and only one permanent custodian.[26] How can the courts make fast decisions in cases where two fit parents each desire custody? Goldstein, Freud, and Solnit advise that in such cases a "drawing of lots" would be the optimal way of choosing the child's custodian. (Interestingly, they do not make a special case for the mother). Once that determination is made, moreover, it should be the custodian who decides if and when the other parent should visit the child. Weiss (1978) has pointed out that the merit of this particular proposition would be in ending the helplessness of custodial parents in dealing with vindictive non-custodial parents. Indeed, the spirit of the Goldstein, Freud, and Solnit recommendations is not controversial. It is aimed at reducing the possibility of a parental tug-of-war in which each parent claims his or her legal rights while tearing the child apart. Goldstein, Freud, and Solnit fail to demonstrate, however, that joint custody actually increases the probability of such struggles. Without citing even an illustrative case history, the authors dismiss joint custody as "an official invitation to erratic changes and discontinuity in the life of the child."

Even if we assume their premises to be true (for example, that a child needs one psychological parent and one home), it would still not be clear that their policy recommendations logically followed. As their critics have pointed out, it is possible that abolishing visitation rights would have an effect opposite to the one intended.[27] That is, the empowered custodial spouse could use visitation to reward or punish the ex-spouse. This situation would allow endless power struggles between divorced parents—struggles that Goldstein, Freud, and Solnit seek to prevent. Another possibility is that parents who could not agree on placement, rather than lose the child entirely, would try to maintain a nonviable marriage. This could result in an escalation of parental discord. Again, the result would be the opposite of the one intended.

On the other side of this issue are Mel Roman and William Haddad who argue in *The Disposable Parent* that joint custody is the optimal postdivorce arrangement and that courts should begin with a presumption for joint custody. Roman and Haddad share with Goldstein, Freud, and Solnit the idea that children need consistency and continuity of affection. The difference is that Roman and Haddad feel that it is precisely joint custody that allows that consistency to continue. To break the bond between the child and one parent arbitrarily is to destroy continuity of care. The authors posit that joint custody allows both adults the gratifications of parenting while eliminating the syndrome of the overwhelmed single parent.

Carol Stack, who has also recommended that courts begin with a presumption for the joint award, maintains that single custody deprives the child of a chance to learn another world view—another approach to problems—from the noncustodial parent.[28] She argues that such exposure better equips children for life in our pluralistic society. Stack also points out that single-parent custody can cut a child off from the entire set of relatives of the other parent. Joint custody, on the other hand, allows the child's support group to expand, including not only both parents and their relatives but also each parent's new friends. Joint custody, therefore, instead of being "no family at all" might resemble the extended family of other societies. It would seem that whereas Goldstein, Freud, and Solnit emphasize the child's vulnerability and its need for a consistent and predictable world, their critics emphasize the child's resilience and its need for stimulation from diverse sources.

Even as of this writing, there has been very little research conducted on joint custody. A pioneering study was performed by Connie Ahrons (1979) on forty-one parents who had been awarded joint custody. She found a broad range of parental relationships—from bitter enemies to best friends—with most parents falling in the middle. Most of the families had arranged for children to reside part of the time with each parent. Ahrons has dubbed this the "binuclear family" because it has two interrelated houses or nuclei. She has pointed out that we will need to develop our language to account for the family forms that will arise with increasing frequency as the divorce and remarriage rates increase.

Greif (1979) also studied fathers, eight of whom had joint custody and thirty-two of whom were visiting parents. Greif used the term *child absence*, analogous to "father absence," to refer to the condition of deprivation caused by the absence of one's children. In contrast to the common conception that fathers walk away from divorce unscathed and carefree, the majority of these men reported severe postdivorce stress. In this study, again, however, there was no assessment of the children.

Questions Addressed by This Investigation

Research on custody to date has raised more questions than it has answered. No study, as of this writing, has compared maternal, parental, and joint custody. The purpose of comparing them here was not to determine which of the three is best but to begin to understand how each of them works.

In response to the judges and mental-health professionals who still believe in maternal instinct, the study posed its first question:

1. Is there any evidence from the measures of child adjustment or family functioning that would support a legal presumption for custody in the mother? The first question gives rise to the second:
2. What are the advantages and disadvantages of maternal, paternal, and joint custody (a) from the adults' point of view and (b) from the children's point of view?

The third question has to do with the process whereby a family transforms itself from one with married parents to one with divorced parents:

3. How do families in the three custody types restructure their daily lives? Another way of asking this is, what constitutes successful coping after divorce?

These questions arose from a particular set of theoretical assumptions about the family and must be understood in the context of those assumptions. Before proceeding to the description of procedures and statistical results, an exploration of the author's theoretical background is offered.

Author's Theoretical Perspective

Gregory Bateson in *Mind and Nature* exhorted scholars to examine what he called our "presuppositions," that is, our ideas about which questions are worth pursuing and our notions of *how* one comes to know the answers. Epistemology, Bateson insists, is always "personal."[29]

American social science has not placed a high priority on examining presuppositions. European psychology has been much more astute at theory building in general and at theoretical self-reflexivity in particular. American psychology, from its beginnings, has focused its genius on problem solving.

What could be an innocuous matter of emphasis (that is, on the pragmatic versus the intellectual) has led to a fallacious extreme. We know from contemporary physics that it is impossible to observe a system without entering and changing it. The search for the grail of "objectivity" in social science has led to clever methods of controlling "observer bias"—typically without regard for how the research question arose in the first place. The outcome of a study is always a result of the question posed, which is itself shaped through a complex transaction between the person of the investigator and the historical period. The social context of research conditions the results infinitely more than the methodological detail (for example, the degree of naïveté of the data coders). Nonetheless, most academic psychologists proceed as though the world of research were "above" politics

> like some abstract Agora where ideas duel gracefully among themselves, unconscious of whose interests they serve.[30]

This social-scientific fallacy, that one can interpret research without considering its cultural birthright, has been dubbed by Diana Hume George, "the myth of mythlessness."

I share Bateson's interest in "presuppositions" and will attempt to make clear the intellectual and social context out of which this research grew.

Theory of the Family

In this study, families' activities are often referred to as family *functions*. Use of this word is not meant to imply affiliation with Functionalism, a sociological theory of family relations developed by Talcott Parsons. While Parsonian theory has made an important contribution to understanding how the parts of a family interconnect to form a homeostasis, it errs in defining the patriarchal nuclear family as the norm. (The definition of a family as necessarily having a sexual division of labor called "instrumental" and "expressive" has already been discussed.) Functionalism is a theory much less concerned with conflict than with harmony, and as such it is incomplete. It cannot explain instances of the family and the individual being fundamentally at odds (for example, the instances in which the family has worked to oppress children and women).

My own presuppositions fit best with critical theory, as developed by Mark Poster in his rigorous and lucid *Critical Theory of the Family*. Critical theory, with its roots in the Frankfurt School, shows a debt both to Marx and to Freud. It is concerned both with the family's historical context and also with the dynamics of its intimate life. It is a theory that acknowledges the ways in which the family can oppress individuals and that therefore supports reform toward the elimination of sex hierarchy and the minimization of age hierarchy. Poster labels his theory "critical" as opposed to "ideological." *Ideological* theories are criticized not because of their political flavor, since all theories are ultimately political, but because they:

> present the social structure ahistorically, as a natural, inevitable, unchangeable or universal feature of human existence. Any theory that tells us what we have is what we must have is ideological.[31]

The theories of Talcott Parsons and Erik Erikson are criticized for their ideological quality.

As a critical theorist, I subscribe neither to the Parsonian doctrine that enshrines the nuclear family (thereby endorsing the hegemony) nor to the view that the family is the root of all evil.[32] People will always need to live in small groups. How small and with what distribution of resources are other questions. This particular view of the family naturally influences the author's theory of investigation, described next.

Theory of Investigation

In the 1940s, the study of the family was considered to be the study of marriage alone. Later attempts, as described in this chapter, tended to focus on individual family members. This study has followed the most current trend, which is to study whole families.

Critical theory emphasizes the need to understand the entire family in its *dailiness*. Relevant questions become: "How does the family earn its living?" "Who controls the checkbook?" "Who cooks?" "How often do grandma and grandpa visit?" "In what ways do the neighborhood and the church support or thwart the family?" The first step thus is to map out who does what, and how they feel about doing it. The next task is to make inferences from this information about: (1) the quality of interpersonal relationships within the family and (2) the family's relationship to the larger social order.

These questions could be asked in a questionnaire, of course, but a questionnaire would not elicit answers with the detail and texture desired. My goal was to describe the phenomenology of three types of families in their daily realities. For this, there is no better instrument than human dialogue.

All scientific endeavors are full of contradictions. This study, for example, was a doctoral dissertation and was therefore designed to accommodate to the traditions of the discipline. Thus a standard test of self-concept was used, as well as analysis of variance, and other techniques associated with positivism.

The quantitative results can be considered as only suggestive of certain trends. The sample size and sampling procedure make it impossible to interpret the statistics literally.

With regard to the content of the study, my expectations were clear and can be shared. Extensive review of the literature had led me to believe that divorce itself was not a cause of childhood psychopathology but that it was instead a life crisis that could lead to higher or lower levels of functioning.[33] It is probable, then, that when I erred in assessing these ninety-one children, I erred in the direction of minimizing pathology.

From the outset I looked favorably on paternal and joint custody insofar as they were signs of dissatisfaction with our too-rigid definitions of acceptable behavior for women and men. However, since men are not socialized to be primary caretakers of children, I wondered if I would not find lower levels of overt support and empathy with children.

With regard to joint custody, the issue of parental conflict was—and is—of central concern. If conflict were the more potent stressor for children, then perhaps the custody decision was best that did not require parents to continue making important decisions together. I could not have predicted that there would be no difference between the conflict levels of joint-custody and single-custody parents.

Finally, I assumed that men and women would face different problems as single parents, but again, could not predict what they would be. I assumed men would have more problems with social stigma because they were operating out of their gender role. I assumed women would have more money problems because they earn less. I was correct about some of these assumptions and incorrect about others.

Limitations of the Study

This study was based on a small sample of people who volunteered to participate for no financial reward. It may be that they represent the healthiest members of the divorced population. Future studies that enjoy more systematic sampling procedures may controvert these findings.

With regard to the interviews, one male lawyer suggested that divorced men would not easily open up to a female investigator. I did not experience a lack of candor on the part of the fathers, but I cannot rule out the possibility that the mothers, because they were more comfortable with me, gave more valid accounts of their situations.

Finally, although the intention of the study was to study entire families, noncustodial parents were not interviewed. In many cases, these parents were considered to be very much a part of the family—particularly by the children. They were excluded from the study for logistical reasons alone. A great number of them lived out of state.

In sum, this is an exploratory study whose aim is more to be hypothesis generating than hypothesis testing (cf. Weiss 1968). I hope that readers will find interesting the accounts from the interviews, and that they will spark ideas for future exploration.

Overview of Study Procedures and
Quantitative Findings

The purpose of this section is to describe briefly the procedures and quantitative findings of this study. The remaining chapters are devoted to exploring data from the interviews with the families.

In the interest of reaching an audience of nonspecialists, most of the research apparatus and details of the results have been confined to appendixes.

The Sample

The sample consisted of sixteen custodial mothers, sixteen custodial fathers, and eighteen parents with joint custody—along with their ninety-one children. In order to qualify for the study, the following had to apply: The family had at least one child under sixteen years; the custodial spouse had not remarried; and the final separation had occurred at least two years prior to the interview.

The goal for recruitment was to find a nonclinical sample of divorced families whose lives had returned to some kind of normalcy. This goal was (partially) ensured by interviewing families after the crisis stage and by not soliciting families from clinics. Other studies have set out to reach a "normal" sample but have either offered participants psychotherapy as part of the "package" (Wallerstein and Kelly 1980) or simply demanded such extensive participation that families might well have volunteered in order to get professional attention (Hetherington, Cox, and Cox 1979). Participation in this study required only one evening. Interviews were conducted in the family's home for their convenience and to remove any associations with treatment that would come from the environment of the university clinic.

The mean time since the final separation for all custody groups was 3.5 years. The average age of the parents at the time of the interview was thirty-seven years (see table A-1 in appendix A). Half of the families belonged to a "high-education" category (that is, four years of college or more) and half belonged to a "low-education" category (that is, two years of college or less).

Families were matched on the number, sex, and age of their children (see table A-2 in appendix A).

Volunteers were recruited from singles' groups, newspaper ads, from lawyers and colleagues, and from each other (see table A-3 in appendix A).

Measures and Results

Child Adjustment. (1) As an indicator of child adjustment, the Piers-Harris Self-Concept Test for Children was administered. This sample did not score any lower on self-concept than the standardized mean. The children's scores also did not differ according to custody type. That is—the self-concept of children in maternal, paternal, and joint custody were not significantly different from each other. However, children's scores *were* significantly lower in families that had sustained high conflict after divorce—regardless of custody type. This finding supports evidence reviewed earlier about the harmful effects of parental discord (see table B-1 in appendix B).

(2) Parents rated their children on a series of items related to the child's behavior problems, psychosomatic problems, and self-esteem (see appendix C). The results were similar to those of the Piers-Harris. Parents' ratings of their children were independent of custody type. In families where parental conflict remained high, however, children had more behavior and psychosomatic problems and lower self-esteem—regardless of custody type (see tables B-2 and B-3 in appendix B). There was a significant correlation between the Piers-Harris scores and the parents' ratings of their children's self-esteem.

Parents were also asked if the children's academic performance had improved, declined, or stayed the same since the final separation. Some children had made better grades and some worse since the separation, but there was no overall trend in either direction. There were also no differences on this variable by custody type.

The Home Atmosphere. A family task was designed in order to assess the quality of the family's interaction. Each family was asked to sit together and invent stories for five TAT cards. Their stories were tape recorded and then coded by an independent rater. The family was rated on the emotional repertoire it displayed in uniting to complete the task. There were no differences in the emotional atmospheres of families headed by men and by women (see appendix C).

Parents' Adjustment. Parents ranked from 1 to 9 (most to least stressful) nine problems they have as single parents (for example, money, disciplining, and loneliness) (see table B-4 in appendix B). This is referred to as the Rank-Stress scale. Parents also rated the level of spouse conflict as they remembered it during the marriage and as it was at the time of the interview. There were no differences in the levels of spouse conflict by custody type. (The conflict scale is included in the interview schedule in appendix C).

Family Functioning. The interview schedule was constructed on the basis of the issues raised in the literature regarding the lives of divorced parents as they perform five tasks: economics, authority, domestics, childcare, and social support.[34] The following chapters report the results of the interviews, which were tape recorded and transcribed. (The interview schedule is contained in appendix C.)

Notes

1. U.S. Bureau of the Census, *Statistical Abstract of the United States* (Washington, D.C.: Government Printing Office, 1977).

2. Bruno Bettelheim, "Fathers Shouldn't Try to Be Mothers," *Parents' Magazine*, October 1956, pp. 124-125.

3. Fitzhugh Dodson, *How to Father* (New York: New American Library, 1977).

4. Ted Klein, *Father and Child* (New York: William Morrow, 1968).

5. James Levine, *Who Will Raise the Children?* (New York: Lippincott, 1976).

6. Avery Corman, *Kramer versus Kramer* (New York: New American Library, 1977).

7. John Irving, *The World According to Garp* (New York: Simon and Schuster, 1979).

8. Benjamin Spock, *Raising Children in a Difficult Time* (New York: Norton, 1974).

9. This phrase comes from the title of a book by Mel Roman and William Haddad, *The Disposable Parent* (New York: Holt, Reinhart and Winston, 1978).

10. *People* v. *Mecein*, 8 Paige Ch. 46, 69, 1839.

11. *Finlay* v. *Finlay*, 148 N.E. at 626, 1925.

12. See Roman and Haddad, *The Disposable Parent*, for a discussion of this issue.

13. *Tuter* v. *Tuter*, 120 S.W. 2d 203, 205 (Ct. App. 1938).

14. *Phillips* v. *Phillips*, 153 Florida, 133, 13 So 2d 922, 1943, p. 135.

15. *Braiman* v. *Braiman*, 44 N.Y. 2d 584, 407 N.Y.S. 2d 449, 378 N.E. 2d 1019 (1978).

16. Henry Foster and Doris Freed, "Joint Custody," *Trial*, June 1980, p. 25.

17. Ibid., p. 26.

18. Lindsy Van Gelder, "Single Mothers—Last of the Supermoms," *Ms. Magazine*, April 1981, p. 47. Reprinted with permission.

19. For a more complete review of this book, see Deborah Luepnitz, "A Review of *Surviving the Break-Up*," *Journal of Marriage and the Family* 43, no. 3 (1981).

20. See J. Santrock and R. Tracy, "Effect of Children's Family Structure Status on the Development of Stereotypes in Teachers," *Journal of Educational Psychology* 70 (1978):754-757. The authors found that teachers rated a child as more disturbed on eleven personality variables when they thought he or she was from a divorced home than when they thought he or she was from an intact home.

21. Alice Rossi, "A Biosocial Perspective on Parenting," *Daedalus*, Spring 1977, pp. 1-31.

22. For a thorough review of this argument, see Nancy Choderow's, *The Reproduction of Mothering* (Berkeley: University of California Press, 1978).

23. I. Broverman, D. Broverman, F. Clarkson, P. Rosenkrantz, and S. Vogel, "Sex-Role Stereotypes and Clinical Judgments of Mental Health," *Journal of Consulting and Clinical Psychology* 34 (1970):1-7.

24. Choderow, *Reproduction of Mothering*, p. 218.

25. Ibid., p. 218.

26. In their most recent book, the authors soften their stance against joint custody somewhat. See Joseph Goldstein, Anna Freud, and Albert J. Solnit, *Before the Best Interests of the Child* (New York: Free Press, 1979).

27. D. Katkin, B. Bullington, and M. Levine, "Above and Beyond the Best Interests of the Child: An Inquiry Into the Relationship Between Social Science and Social Action," *Law and Society Review*, Summer 1974, pp. 669-689.

28. Carol Stack, "Who Owns the Child? Divorce and Custody Decisions in Middle-Class Families," *Social Problems* 23 (1976):505-515.

29. Gregory Bateson, *Mind and Nature* (New York: Dutton, 1979). Bateson, ironically, did not devote much time to examining *his* presuppositions. Systems theory thus remains vague and ahistorical. Scholars of diverse schools find some "systems" principles useful, but systems theory alone remains too thin to stand without the scaffolding of, say, structuralism, psychoanalysis, or critical theory.

30. Lilian Robinson, *Sex, Class and Culture* (Bloomington: Indiana University Press, 1978), p. 5.

31. Mark Poster, *Critical Theory of the Family* (New York: Seabury Press, 1978), p. xix.

32. David Cooper, *The Death of the Family* (New York: Vintage Books, 1971).

33. D. Aguilera and J. Messick, *Crisis Intervention: Theory and Methodology* (Saint Louis: Mosby, 1974). Crisis theory is compatible with critical theory because they share the dialectical notion of growth through conflict.

34. R. Brandwein, C. Brown, and E. Fox, "Women and Children Last: The Social Situation of Divorced Mothers and their Families," *Journal of Marriage and the Family* 36 (1974):498-514. My use of these five categories was influenced by the authors' use of similar categories.

2

The Custody and Visitation Arrangements

This chapter deals with issues related to custody and visitation. It was important to find out what types of arrangements the mothers, fathers, and joint-custody parents had originally desired and how they had gone about securing those arrangements. Did they consult with professionals in making their plans? Did they consult their children? How satisfied with their arrangements were both children and adults at the time of the interview?

The issues that arose in making these decisions were somewhat different for the joint-custody families. To avoid confusion, the joint families will be discussed separately in the final section of this chapter. We begin with a consideration of single-custody mothers and fathers.

How the Mothers Attained Custody

The modal response of the mothers to the question of how they chose full custody was, "It was never a question; it was just assumed that I would have the children." Seventy-five percent of the mothers made this the essence of their explanation. When pressed on why this had been assumed, the mothers mentioned a variety of factors, for example, their husbands did not want the children or the husbands were less competent parents. Many of the mothers felt that they had a right to custody, based on their having carried the primary if not exclusive responsibility for the children during the marriage. Here is a case in point:

> **Mother:** There was no problem in deciding on custody. It was just assumed I would have them.
> **I:** Why was it assumed?
> **Mother:** Well, if anyone has a right to have them, it's me. I raised them. He spent maybe a few minutes a week with them. . . . But it never came up, even in passing. It's like your right arm. (Therapy aid, children are ten and fifteen.)

Approximately one-third of the mothers mentioned that they could not have pulled through emotionally without the children and that that factor was part of their reason for wanting custody. One mother put it this way:

> He is an excellent parent, but they are the most important thing in my life, and I would not have survived without them. They would have been happy

either way, but I wouldn't have pulled through if I had lost them. (Graduate student and secretary, children are fifteen and sixteen.)

Mothers were asked if they would have been willing to relinquish custody if their ex-husbands had expressed such a desire. One mother said she had been tempted to relinquish custody in order to pursue her career. She had decided this would not have been best for the children, however. Here are her words:

> I have considered relinquishing them. I consider it every time I get into self pity and think I'm going to be twenty-eight years old and haven't even started college. I had planned to have my Master's degree by now and be in private practice. I haven't got anything yet. He has offered to take them so I can do my own thing. That would be great for me if he were a stable person. He lives on 10 mg of valium a day and is an alcoholic. As hard as it is, I am by far the superior parent. (Unemployed mother, children are six and nine.)

The next question was if they would have considered *sharing* custody had their ex-husbands been willing. One mother reported that she had asked her lawyer about joint custody because she felt the children wanted to maintain a close relationship with both parents. She said that her lawyer "brusquely dismissed the question with a, 'No, you don't want anything like that.' " She did not pursue it, lest she appear not to want her children. Many of the mothers in the sample had not heard of joint custody, or they had only a vague notion of its meaning. When I described it, 43 percent of the mothers said they would have been willing to try some form of shared custody if their ex-spouses had been willing. An additional 37 percent would have been willing if their ex-husbands had been "fit parents." This would seem to suggest that we can expect joint custody to become more popular as it becomes more visible to people through the media and as more lawyers come to see it as a viable alternative.

How the Fathers Attained Custody

There were some clear differences in the ways mothers and fathers attained custody. For example, there were twice as many legal contests over custody among paternal as among maternal families (25 percent versus 12 percent). In an additional 19 percent of paternal cases, there was a bitter struggle over custody, which was settled out of court. In nearly half of the paternal families, the children had been initially in the custody of their mothers. Most of these children were turned over to their fathers explicitly because their mothers felt incompetent to care for them. Here is an example:

After a couple of months, my ex-wife called me up in tears and asked me to take the kids. She couldn't handle them. She had little money and couldn't manage working and watching them too. She was having problems with welfare and with sitters. She had never been on her own before. She was only sixteen when we got married, and it was all too much for her. (Forklift operator, children are three and six.)

In one case, the mother had agreed to relinquish custody of her daughter, until her lawyer pressured her to use it as a bargaining chip:

My ex-wife had always said she didn't want custody. But then her lawyer told her, "What! You've got to use custody to get money!" She took our daughter and moved out of state for seven months. They got 90 percent of their material demands, and I finally got custody. (Business executive, daughter is seven.)

One father who had had to fight for custody in court stated that it had cost him $10,000:

I had to take out a loan, and my parents had to take out a loan. But it was worth it. I would have done anything to get my children back. It was hell for me those eight months while they were with her. I was worried to death about them. They all told the judge they wanted their Dad, and the judge decided because of her drinking and running around that I was the better parent. (Plumber, children are eight, thirteen, and fourteen.)

Another father said he could not bear to think of what the custody of his children had cost him, as it had involved *several* battles in court. This father was separated seven years prior to the interview, when presumably the courts were less favorably disposed to fathers than they are now.

When I first went to my lawyer, he said that no judge in this area would award custody to a father. When I would go to visit the kids, they would be gone, so I took her to court and she moved with the kids to Nevada where they were in hiding for four months. We went to court and the judge switched the kids to me because of her actions. But she won an appeal and took the kids to New York. The kids have been in five different junior high schools. We went to court five times over whether she could take the kids and disappear—and she did what she wanted anyway. She told the judge to jump in a lake. If I had done what she's done I would be in Attica. . . . A couple of years later, out of the blue, she decided she couldn't get along with them anymore, and sent them to live with me. (Psychiatrist, children are fifteen and sixteen.)

It is not surprising that this father's children scored two of the lowest self-concept scores in the sample on the Piers-Harris. Both children appeared withdrawn during the interview.

In approximately one-third of the paternal families, the custody decision had been made without acrimony—and in one case, quite amicably. Here is a quote from that case:

> During the marriage we had both worked and both cared for Josh. Actually I was closer to him and did more for him than she. She was determined not to be a traditional mother and isn't. She has moved East to follow her profession. There was a tacit assumption all along that I would have him. (Professor, son is seven.)

In summary, it would appear as though the children in this study who were in paternal custody had endured a more difficult experience than those who were in maternal custody. Half of the paternal children had undergone a change of custody from mother to father, and many of them had been involved in court battles over their custody. Thus, if there had been a difference in their adjustment scores, it would have been difficult to interpret. As described in chapter 1, however, no differences were found on any of the adjustment measures between children in maternal and paternal custody.

Who Helped in Making the Custody Decision

More fathers than mothers consulted with professionals about custody. One-third of the men reported that they discussed custody issues with their lawyers, and one-quarter of them consulted psychologists. In contrast, only 20 percent of the mothers discussed custody with a professional—in each case, their lawyer. The fathers had high praise for the people who helped them. One father said that for several weeks during the custody fight, he spoke to his lawyer for fifteen minutes every morning, just for support and encouragement! More fathers than mothers were satisfied with their lawyers. The difference may be due to the fact that one-third of the fathers had a lawyer who was a personal friend. Women—particularly homemakers—are less likely to have friends who are lawyers. This issue is discussed again in chapter 3 on economics.

Consulting Children about Custody

Dr. Lee Salk, in his popular *What Every Child Would Like His Parents to Know About Divorce,* noted that the most common question parents ask him about custody is whether or not the decision should be left up to the children. His own opinion is that the *final* choice should never be made by the child—that it should be made by parents (or judges, if necessary). This, he feels, should be made explicit to the child, to attenuate anxiety he or she may feel about having to choose between parents. Salk does believe, however, that some degree of participation in the custody decision is appropriate and may be even helpful in giving the child some sense of control over what is happening in the family. It was interesting to compare his position with the reports of parents and childen in the study.

Children in Maternal Custody

Only a few children in maternal custody had been asked with whom they wanted to live after divorce. Each child reported that the decision had been painful. The other maternal children simply were told by their parents with whom they would live. This is consistent with the fact that, in the maternal cases, custody was assumed and not discussed even between the spouses. Among the children who were not consulted, half said they were glad they had not been given a choice because it would have been terribly difficult. Here are two examples of this position:

> I: If they had asked you, what would you have said?
> C: I would have said I wanted to live with both—not either one—both.
> I: But if they had asked you . . .
> C: I wouldn't have said either. 'Cause I love them both. (Girl, seven.)

The comments of an adolescent boy were similar:

> They didn't ask me, and I'm glad they didn't. It would have meant hurting one of them. I'm close to both of them in different ways. I'm glad they didn't put that responsibility on me. (Boy, twelve.)

It is worth noting, nonetheless, that half of the children felt they would have had no trouble in choosing their custodian. Here is the comment of one such child:

> C: No, it wouldn't have been hard. I would definitely have said my mom.
> I: Why?
> C: He left mom because he didn't like her. I'm kind of mad at him for that! (Boy, twelve.)

Children in Paternal Custody

One-third of the children from paternal families had been asked their preference about custody. Note that the parents felt that this was a meaningful question that would help them decide where the child would live; it was not done merely for form's sake. Among this third of children who had been consulted, nearly all reported that the choice had been difficult. The accounts of fathers and children on the question of whether or not children were consulted were consistent with each other. That is, there was no case in which a father said "We consulted our child" and the child reported otherwise. But parents who *did* confer with their children on custody tended to understate the difficulty with which the child made the decision. For example, a thirteen-year-old boy described the process in this way:

> They asked me. I didn't know what to do. I figured my best bet was to stay out here where my friends are. It took me a few weeks to decide. I had been trying not to think about it. One night the whole family went to counseling so I could decide where to live. The counselor went over the facts—no pressure. My parents tried not to pressure me—but they did a little—kind of being buddy-buddy. (Boy, thirteen.)

I asked this child's father, a physician, what the process of deciding on custody had been like for his son. The father replied, "I don't think it was much of a decision at all. Greg just assumed he would be living with me." Similarly, a father said that his son's decision had been clear-cut because "He doesn't get along well with his mother. And besides—he's been Dad's boy since we brought him home from the hospital." The child's account, however, revealed conflict:

> My dad asked me where I wanted to live. I had told him early on I wanted to live with him. It was hard. How could I tell my mom that? I didn't move out because I didn't love my mother—only because I wanted to live here. (Boy, fourteen.)

In a third case, a mother mentioned that her daughter had had a "passing thought" about living with her father and that she would have been free to do so. The daughter, however, reported that she had wanted very much to switch but that her mother had cried and "guilt tripped" her out of it.

With regard to Salk's recommendations, we have no way of knowing if being consulted on the custody question ultimately helped these children to cope with the divorce. It is fairly clear in the cases presented here that the children found the decision painful indeed. The most important result to emerge from this section is that at least one-half of the children who were asked to choose between their parents suffered in a way that their parents—perhaps preoccupied with their own distress—failed to notice.

Parents' Satisfaction with Custody

All the mothers and fathers said they were happy to be custodial parents, and none was interested in changing the custodial arrangement. Parents were asked, "What are the advantages and disadvantages of having custody of your children?"

Fathers had a much easier time with this question than mothers, whose answers were less elaborate and sometimes strained. Said one mother:

> When you're a mother, there is no such question. You have children and you raise them because you love them, and it's not a question of advantages and disadvantages. (Store manager, son is fifteen.)

Almost all the mothers mentioned that one advantage of single motherhood was that there was less conflict than in marriage and that their children were growing up outside of that chaos. One mother put it this way:

> It's nice not having to put up with stuff from him. Mindy saw a lot of violence between us. He always insisted on doing it in front of her rather than waiting. She would get hysterical when this happened. So she's much better off without that nightmare. And I'm better off, too. I can discuss my feelings and problems as a parent with my friends. They may not have the same investment as her father, but I get better suggestions from them. (History professor, daughter is seven.)

Other advantages mentioned were: "It is personally satisfying to raise them," "With me I know they're in good hands," and "They are good company for me." It was evident in the interview that mothers had a hard time with these questions. Their answers were terse in comparison with the fathers'. This is consistent with the fact that so many of the mothers had simply assumed that they would be the custodian and had never stopped to weigh the costs and benefits of taking custody. Many of the fathers, on the other hand, had actually *been* noncustodial parents for a short while and could compare the conditions of being custodial and noncustodial. Here are some typical comments:

> The advantages of custody? The companionship, the love, the hugging and kissing, the sharing of experiences, trips, things we do together. Living alone is interesting for a while, but it wears out fast. There's no one to talk to. (School principal, children are twelve and fourteen.)

Said another father:

> Being invited to mother's day plays. The special things done for me by the kids. They were a great support to me when I was freshly divorced. I've talked to fellas who don't have their children and listen to them talk about coming home from work to an empty apartment and being bored with going out. When I leave work I say, "I wonder what's going on at home tonight." It's great having a family. (Machinist, children are eleven, twelve, and fourteen.)

Other reasons mentioned were similar to the mothers', that is, the absence of conflict, the personal satisfaction, and the knowledge that they are in good hands. The only different response was that fathers mentioned that it is cheaper to raise children in one's own house than to pay the ex-spouse to support them. Fully half of the fathers spontaneously cited this as an advantage. The reason was that paying the ex-spouse to support them meant including a share of her rent and utilities as part of the child's expenses.

In terms of the disadvantages of having custody, approximately 80 percent of both mothers and fathers reported that there are times when single parenting is overwhelming. The modal response of fathers on this issue was "You can't come and go as you please," whereas mothers talked about the exhaustion and worry from having full responsibility for children. The comment of this mother is illuminating:

> It is lonely being a single parent. It is a heavy responsibility. I used to want to run away right after the divorce; the kids were driving me nuts. I couldn't have a private life. I had to work nights because of them. All I wanted was some time off, yet I felt guilty about sending my son to stay with his father for the summer. But that's their father—why should I feel that way? He's a good parent. I felt uneasy but I finally did take a vacation. The kids loved it! Why did I torture myself! (LPN, children are four and eight.)

Other mothers' complaints were similar:

> It seems overwhelming at times. I'm the only one to sit up with her all night when she's sick. (History professor, daughter is seven.)

Another mother worried:

> Making decisions about them is hard. I find myself saying, "Would he approve of this?" (Unemployed mother, children are eleven, thirteen, and fourteen.)

The fathers also felt that single custody had its disadvantages, but their emphasis was different. The accounts of the fathers on this subject stress the difficulty of carrying on an active social life while raising children alone. The fact that fathers in the sample dated more than mothers is one reason for the difference in emphasis. Said one father:

> One thing I looked forward to as a single person was going out again. My friends who are single but don't have their children live a life very different from mine. Some of them dedicate their entire after-five existence to partying. Not that I'd want to do that—but it is a pain always to have to get sitters. And it's expensive too. Also, I feel I should spend some of my weekend with the kids, 'cause I'm the only parent they got. (Mechanic, daughters are four, eight, twelve, and thirteen.)

Another father said, in a similar vein:

> The main disadvantage of having custody is not being able to come and go
> as you please. Sometimes I would just like to go to a movie at the last
> minute, or go to join someone for a drink, but with a baby to take care of,
> it's impossible. It seems like every thing I do socially has to be planned at
> least a week in advance. (Architect, son is three.)

Anxiety over Losing Custody

Parents were asked if they ever feared that their ex-spouse could return to
court and win a fight for full custody of the children. Only one mother but
one-third of the fathers reported that they feared this possibility. Here is a
statement from the mother who worried that her ex-husband, who was
politically well connected, might try to get custody of their son to punish her
for the divorce:

> I have always been afraid that he could go to court and get my son. His
> family is wealthy and they have put several public officials in power, and
> removed others. He has been so remiss about visiting Daniel, however, that
> I am beginning to feel more confident that he couldn't possibly make a
> case. (Secretary, son is four.)

Several men feared that their ex-wives could win a custody appeal because
of the courts' presumption for the mother.

> I did worry about that and I suppose I still do. I live a pretty clean way of
> life and feel to some extent in a glass bowl. Since then she has lost custody
> of her other son too—to the child's father. That makes it a bit safer for me.
> It's not like I live in terror—but there is something that's always there. (Ar-
> chitect, son is three.)

Said another father:

> F: One of my biggest fears is her going after Marty. Whenever I do some-
> thing that's not strictly kopasetic—I'm nervous that she could get him.
> I: Could she prove you unfit?
> F: I don't think so.
> I: How does your fear affect your behavior?
> F: A couple of times the woman I date has spent the night here with her
> daughter. I don't know exactly what the law states, but I worry if she could
> go to court and say that I entertain women in my home in front of my son.
> (Salesman, son is fifteen.)

Finally, here are the comments of a father who was so worried that he
would not leave his children alone for five minutes without getting a sitter:

I've always been afraid that she could get them back. It's a scarey thing because they are doing well now. Even though she is an alcoholic, I know that judges prefer children to be with their mothers. Sometimes I worry that if they spend too much time visiting her that the bond will become closer and she will want them back. (Machinist, children are eleven, twelve, and fourteen.)

This father was very frank in admitting that his insecurities about custody prevent him from encouraging the children to visit their mother often. His feelings are understandable and probably not uncommon.

Children's Satisfaction with Custody

The children in the sample were basically satisfied with their custodial placement. Only one paternal child and three maternal children reported that they would have changed the custody arrangement to live with the other parent if they had the chance. One of these children had, in fact, been given permission to switch. He is a boy who had seen his dad on weekends during the seven years since his parents separated. He had this to say:

I have decided to live with my dad. We don't know each other well and I want to know him better. I wanted to switch for a while but hesitated because I didn't want to leave my mom alone. She told me it was all right. It took me a month to decide. We will stay close. (Boy, fifteen).

In addition to the four who definitely wanted to switch custodians, there were also ten paternal children and nine maternal children who said that they "sometimes wished" they lived with their other parent—although not to the extent that they would switch if given a chance. What were their reasons? Three-quarters of them stated unequivocally that this was based not on a desire to leave one parent but on a desire to be with the other parent. Here is a comment from a boy living with his mother:

I would like to live with them both. But since I can't, Mom is good, because I'd have to move out all my toys and I would be far from school. Sometimes I'd like to live with my Dad, but that's because I've lived with Mom so long. If I lived with Dad, then I'd wish I lived with Mom. Get what I mean? But I see him a lot, so it's no use moving. (Boy, nine.)

There was one teenaged girl who said she would prefer to live with her father but who felt too guilty to move:

I get along with my father better. My mother and I fight all the time. I thought about moving in with him last summer. My mother said I was free to go, but she cried for three days about it. My brother is going away to school, and she would be home alone. I don't know what I'll do yet. (Girl, sixteen.)

Finally, here is an account from a child who cannot switch from father to mother because her mother will not have her:

I would like to be living with my mother right now. But no way. My father would let me go—sure. But she doesn't want the responsibility. Not because I don't like living here—but because I miss my mother. But she left so she could have her freedom. She explained it to me; she's never been on her own. I can understand. I think she's selfish, but I can understand why she needs to do her own thing for awhile. (Girl, fifteen.)

Considering the number of children who wished that they lived with their other parent at times, it is not surprising that a number of children were dissatisfied with the amount of visitation they had. This issue is addressed next.

Visitation

The Arrangements

In order to discuss the issue of visitation, parents and children were asked how often the children saw their noncustodial parents. There was no discrepancy between the accounts of parents and children on the amount of visitation.

Twelve types of visitation were enumerated by the sample. These types were categorized for convenience into five groups: no visitation, rare, occasional, frequent, and continuous. (These categories are defined in table D-1 in appendix D.) Less than half the children in the study visit their noncustodial parent frequently or continuously. The majority sees the noncustodian only occasionally or less (see table 2-1).

In all cases, the legal agreement was for frequent or continuous visitation (as defined here). What are the reasons for the disparity between legal and actual amounts of visitation?

First, a careful look at table 2-1 will show that these reasons must be considered separately for the maternal and paternal children because the visitation patterns are very different. In the case of the maternal children, we see a bimodal pattern of visitation. That is, the noncustodial father either visits frequently or he visits very little. The middle category, "occasional," is the smallest.

For the paternal children, the situation is different. If the noncustodial mother does not visit frequently, she visits at least occasionally. The

Table 2-1

Percentage of Maternal and Paternal Children in Five Visitation Patterns

| Custody | Type of Visitation | | | | | |
	None	Rare	Occasional	Frequently	Continuous	Total
Maternal	23.5%	23.5%	9%	41%	3%	100%
(*n*)	(8)	(8)	(3)	(14)	(13)	34
Paternal	6%	19%	31%	44%	—	100%
	(2)	(6)	(10)	(14)	—	32

Note: The maternal- and paternal-custody families show a different distribution of visitation arrangements.
$X^2(4) = 22; p < .001$

category "no visitation" is nearly empty. Noncustodial mothers are much less likely to give up all contact with their children than are noncustodial fathers.

Why do noncustodial fathers stop visiting their children? In half of the cases where the noncustodial father visits rarely or never, it is because the children dislike him and have decided not to see him. But in many other cases, custodial mothers reported that their ex had "split the scene" in order to evade support payments. Indeed, 38 percent of the noncustodial fathers who visited rarely or less paid nothing to their ex-wives, whereas *no* father who visited occasionally or more paid nothing. In the remaining 12 percent of maternal cases, the father lived out of town, which made it logistically difficult to visit.

Why did noncustodial mothers visit less than their legal limit? In the one case where the children never see their mother, it is because of the children's alienation from her (that is, it was their choice). In the cases in which noncustodial mothers visited rarely, their ex-husbands explained that these women had lost interest in their children. (Recall that this disinterest was one reason these fathers had received custody in the first place). This was also exacerbated by the fact that half of the mothers had left town, making it logistically difficult to visit.

Noncustodial parents were not interviewed in this study. It is thus impossible really to understand why they visited their children so little. Even in cases where the custodial parent complained that the ex-spouse had "disappeared," we do not know what the custodian might have done to make the other parent feel excluded. One father (quoted earlier in this chapter) reported that when his wife had custody, he would arrive at her house for visits and discover that the children were not home. This undermining of the visitation by the custodian for the purpose of punishing the ex-spouse is familiar to clinicians who work with divorced families. There are fathers who, in exasperation, *do* give up trying to see their children. There are non-custodial mothers who are made to feel so ashamed about having "abandoned" their children that they find it less painful to leave the situation completely.

Recent literature in the field (especially Wallerstein and Kelly 1980) has emphasized the importance of continued involvement with the noncustodial parent for the child's psychological well-being. Further investigation of why visitation declines over time would be useful indeed.

Children's Feelings about Visitation

How did children feel about visiting the other parent occasionally or less? Approximately half of these children desired more visitation and half desired the same amount or even less. As for the children who already had frequent or continuous visitation, approximately 60 percent were content with that amount, and 40 percent desired even more.

Why do children desire more or less visitation than they have? Did children dread visits because parents used those occasions to fight? Did they want more visitation because the other parent lavished gifts on them? This leads to the question of quality of contact time.

Children who desired less visitation had very clear reasons. These reasons centered on personal antagonisms with the other parent. In the majority of cases, the child has been "turned off" to the noncustodial parent because the latter continued to place the child in the middle of the parents' differences. Here is an example:

> I: Would you like to see your dad more or less?
> C: Never!
> I: Why?
> C: Because he makes mean faces and says things about Mom, and you get sick when you go with him.
> I: You get sick?
> C: Yah. I used to like to go before he started asking the questions.
> C: What questions?
> C: About Mom. Like if she goes with men, and if she works, and if she leaves us with sitters. (Girl, seven.)

This little girl was not exaggerating about getting sick during visits. Her mother reported that she would vomit routinely before or during the visits, out of anxiety that he would not bring them home. Visitation has now stopped.

Those who rarely saw their noncustodial parent were not as specific about their reasons for wanting more contact. Typically, the child explained simply that it hurt when the other children talked about their fathers or mothers. Here is an example:

C: I've only seen him three times since the divorce four years ago. I would like to see him more. I have written him, but he didn't write back. I miss him.
I: What exactly do you miss?
C: I don't know.
I: What kind of thing would make you think about your dad and miss him?
C: I don't know. Just other kids talk about their fathers.
I: Are there things you and he did together?
C: No. (Boy, twelve.)

This quotation raises the next question of exactly what children do with their noncustodial parent on a visit.

How the Visit Is Spent

In approximately half of the maternal and paternal families, children reported spending visits either as a day of treats or as a day to visit their friends in the old neighborhood. Only half of the children described contact with the parent that included some kind of personal sharing. Here are examples of each of the three patterns:

C. We go to the beach and get ice cream and go out to dinner and then he takes me home!
I: Do you enjoy those visits?
C: Uh hunh!
I: Do you have to make your bed and clear the table like here?
C: Nope. (Girl, seven.)

This thirteen-year-old boy illustrates the second pattern—that of visiting the old neighborhood:

C: When I go there, I go in and say hello to her and then go and see my old friends. I take off on my bike and never go back to the house.
I: Do you ever sit down and talk to your mom?
C: No, she just cries and complains about my dad.
I: Do you do any chores around there?
C: Not really.

The third pattern is one in which the child seems to have maintained a meaningful relationship with the noncustodian:

We talk mostly. We talk about school and stuff. About problems or just anything. We watch TV. Sometimes we go to a museum. I'll do some work, like help her wash the car. It's not really different from before the divorce—it's just less time. (Boy, thirteen.)

The last quote is very similar to the response to that question of the joint-custody children. Before comparing the single-custody visit with the conditions of joint custody, however, some background on the joint families is necessary.

The Joint-Custody Families

The Arrangements

Definitions of *joint custody* were various. No two joint arrangements in the sample were identical. Here is a crude breakdown of the eleven arrangements: (1) Children split the week between parents (eight cases); (2) children split the day between their parents (one case); (3) children split the year between parents (one case); and (4) children alternate years with parents (one case). Following is a full description of some of the arrangements:

Splitting the Week. *Joint family A:* "I pick the children up on Saturday morning, and they are with me through Monday. I put them in school on Tuesday and their mother picks them up from school and keeps them through Friday." Thus father has them three days, and mother, four. Each parent has one full weekend per month. *Joint family D:* "The children live with me during the week, and they spend the weekend with their father. In addition, each daughter spends either Tuesday or Wednesday evening alone with her father."

Splitting the Day. *Joint family C:* "During the summer I pick them up after work and they spend the evening here from five to nine P.M. He picks them up at nine P.M., and they sleep there so he can take them for their swimming lesson in the morning. They spend Friday with their father and I pick them up Saturday at two P.M., and they go back Sunday at nine P.M. On winter nights, they spend half the nights here and half there."

Splitting the Year. *Joint family F:* "The kids spend three months of summer and one week at Christmas and Easter with their mother. Otherwise they are here."

Alternating Years. *Joint family H:* "We have had a variety of arrangements depending on where each of us was living. Last year she lived with her mother, and this year she is with me, and next year she'll be with her mom again. We haven't planned beyond that. She spends the summer with the other parent."

The Unstructured Arrangement

Joint family G: "We don't have a structure and never have. The kids had been based with me for several years, and now they have been based with their father for several years. The other parent is always free to drop by any time during the week and has always done so. We both go out of town on consulting jobs often—several times a month. When he goes to Chicago next week, I will move in to stay with the kids. He used to do the same thing. The adults have done most of the switching between houses—not the kids." (This family obviously is not without structure, but they *were* impressively flexible. Because they liked referring to their lifestyle as "unstructured," I have labeled it as such in this book.)

One additional distinction will be made at the outset. It has become convenient to classify the joint families in this study into two groups—one in which joint custody is working to everyone's satisfaction ($N = 8$) and the other in which it is disliked by at least one family member ($N = 3$). The latter will be referred to as the *problematic* joint families and are labeled X, Y, and Z.

Deciding on Joint Custody

How did parents decide on joint custody? In six of the eleven cases, there was no conflict about joint custody; it was always "assumed" that there would be some form of shared custody, based on the couple's having shared parenting during the marriage. In the other joint cases, there was conflict over custody described as "bitter" and "vehement." In one of those cases, there was an actual legal contest. In the others, the parents were able to work out an agreement out of court.

What were parents' reasons for wanting joint custody? Mothers and fathers routinely expressed the following sentiments: "The children need both of us," "We both need the children," "It is unfair for the other parent to be a visitor," and "It is more practical to share custody because we both work." The parents' own accounts are interesting. First, here are the comments of one mother who had had to do some difficult negotiating with her husband over joint custody:

> We wanted to split up, but you can't split two children. Jack couldn't be a visitor to the children—and I couldn't either. It got to one point where I wanted full custody just out of resentment for him. And also it was—how would I be seen by society if I let go of my children? That bothered me a lot, and I had no support from either set of parents. . . . I considered a custody battle, but then I thought—what if I lost? You get some Catholic judge in there, and what if he decides that having had an affair makes me a

bad mother? And besides, I couldn't fight that dear man. (Joint mother B, art historian, children are five and nine, split week.)

Here is her ex-husband's account of their decision:

The reason was—neither of us was willing to give up the kids. We had both parented them equally. But the process was long and bitter. For a while, when we were angry, each of us wanted full custody. My reasons were: I am a better parent. Temperamentally she is too much of a perfectionist and makes demands on them. I am more openly affectionate with them. I spend most of the time they're here doing things with them—messing around in the garden, or this morning we went to a garage sale. She lets them do their own thing. Anyway, we were in a deadlock, and the lawyer suggested joint custody. . . . Then it was a matter of logistics, but once the angry phase had cooled, we both expressed commitment to sharing custody. (Joint father B, college administrator, children are five and nine, split week.)

Here are some comments from people who assumed from the beginning that they would share custody:

We had a political commitment to evade the traditional plan where it was just the mother who had the kids. We had friends who had worked out a joint agreement that was impressive. So we had a model. We wanted them to have the benefit of both houses. We've done a lot of renegotiating over the years to fit the academic calendar. (Joint father D, professor, daughters are twelve and fourteen, split week.)

Here is his ex-wife's account of the decision for joint custody:

I wanted to go back to school after the separation and then work full time, and I thought it would be better for me and for the kids if we shared the responsibility. Also he had had a vasectomy, and it wasn't fair to him not to see these kids since he couldn't have any more. I needed his help in child rearing because of my schooling. At first he had said—go do your own thing; I'll take the kids. He felt guilty about causing the divorce and wanted to do me a favor. I said I needed time to think about everything. Soon he moved out and right away the kids started moving back and forth between houses. We didn't use the word *joint* then. They certainly wanted to be with both of us, and we both wanted them. I can't think of a better arrangement. (Joint mother D, nurse, daughters are twelve and fourteen, split week.)

Another joint mother emphasized not wanting to end up like other single parents she had seen:

I belonged to Parents Without Partners when we first split. I couldn't see myself overwhelmed with all that responsibility when he wanted so much to share custody. That feeling of being trapped that other women felt was not for me! Plus the kids need and love him. Plus I couldn't see going out socially and hiring a sitter when they could be with their father. Things were angry at first. We didn't sit right down and say "joint custody." It evolved. (Joint mother C, researcher, daughters are nine and ten, split day.)

A most noteworthy finding was that fully 60 percent of the joint mothers described hesitation about joint custody because of the feeling that it is not socially acceptable for a mother to "give up" her children. We can learn something about how fathering is viewed in this culture from the fact that the mothers felt that sharing custody with father constituted "giving them up." One mother actually maintained legal custody in her name for that reason, although she and her ex have the most "shared" form of custody in the sample (that is, children split the day). Her ex-husband understood her reservations:

She wanted it in her name legally because of the social acceptability. I couldn't see any good reason to cause a commotion over it. (Joint father C, accountant, daughters are nine and ten, split day.)

This father, nonetheless, along with all the other joint parents, maintained that it was important to him to think of himself as a joint parent and not as a visitor with extended visitation rights. Here are some comments on this point:

It felt very important to me to have joint custody written into the agreement. That means that both parents will have equal roles in raising the child, and that is what we both wanted. It would have seemed completely incongruous for me to go from parent to Sunday visitor. (Join father G, orchestra musician, daughter is nine, alternating years.)

Again the social-acceptability issue emerged:

I feel much more comfortable saying I have joint custody than saying I'm a visiting parent. I was raised Irish Catholic. There was something wrong with a woman who didn't marry and have kids. And you don't leave them. It's a relief not to have them all the time. But when I feel good, I feel guilty. (Joint mother X, social worker with five children, split week.)

The ambivalence that many joint-custody mothers felt can be explained partially in terms of the sexual hierarchy of the larger social order. In a society in which women have little power in the public domain, they will be understandably reluctant to relinquish power in the private sphere. Women expressed in a variety of ways their hesitation in "giving up" their children. Some mothers talked of having a "right" to their children because they had raised them. Other women focused on the disapproval they would meet in the eyes of society if they did not receive full custody. This issue of women's sharing motherhood with men in a society that does not support equal parenting by both sexes is discussed in depth by Diane Ehrensaft.[1]

Consultation about the Custody Decision

Only one joint parent discussed custody with a counselor. This was mother X, quoted previously, who needed to do a lot of thinking in order to "leave behind" her five children.

Lawyers. Nearly all the joint families had discussed joint custody with their lawyers. In fact, in three of the eleven cases, the lawyer had suggested joint custody as an option for parents who were both competent and desirous of custody. But in three other cases, the lawyer was set against joint custody and tried to talk parents out of agreements that they had already completed. In a fourth case, a judge tried to dissuade parents from joint custody, even though they had been practicing it for two and a half years during the separation! Their lawyer explained to the judge that the parents had both been trained as counselors, that both were devoted to their children, and that all family members had felt satisfied with the arrangement they had had. The judge warned that "joint custody is no custody at all!" but the parents were granted the joint award.

Friends. Four families mentioned the support they received from friends— particularly those who had already gone through divorce and who could thus offer empathic suggestions. The D family was creative in including a third party in all their negotiations. The third party was Mr. D's sister who mediated many of their discussions over the years:

> In the beginning we were still into being angry and dumping on each other, so it was not the best frame of mind in which to sit down and make decisions about when the kids would go where. My sister was up at the time, and she was close to both of us. It happened that she sat in on those negotiations to help both of us. She would help clarify issues and move us on when we were just being nasty. Each semester we had to renegotiate the schedule because I would have a night class or she would have a woman's group. My sister continued to sit in on those negotiations, and it worked out great. (Joint father D, professor, daughters are nine and ten, split week.)

Children in the joint families were consulted even less than in cases of single custody. No joint child had been asked her or his preference. Joint parents felt either that the children were too young or that the decision would place too great a burden on them. It is also true, however, that in each joint family with teenagers, the joint schedule revolved around the teens' schedule. These older children were likely to initiate contact with the other parent as well as call off a night in order to attend a party. Parents were proud of this flexibility.

Satisfaction with Joint Custody

Parents' Satisfaction. *The Advantages of Joint Custody.* The major themes that emerged from parents' comments on the advantages of joint custody are similar to their reasons for wanting joint custody in the first place: (1) It gives children the continued benefit of two parents; (2) it gives parents who desire and need their children the chance to remain a part of their lives; (3) parents get a break in order to rest and pursue their own interests; and (4) it is practical in terms of childcare because the children stay with the other parent instead of with sitters. Here are some parents' comments elaborating on these themes:

> The kids were able to maintain as normal a life as possible—as close to the family as it would have been. We modeled to them a value that people can collaborate even when they hate each other. I think it says to them—we really care about you. This has equipped them to deal with change in their own lives. They are very flexible. (Joint mother G, occupational therapist, children are eleven and fifteen, "unstructured.")

Said another joint mother:

> The kids see us as a foursome. Matt brings home pictures from school of all four of us. He even said to one kid, "You have one house; we have two!" And one of our friends has a kid age seven who said to her divorced parent, "Why don't you buy a house down the street so we could see each other more often?" The kids promote this arrangement! (Joint mother B, art historian, children are five and nine, split week.)

Another joint mother emphasized the benefits for the adults:

> It's extremely useful to have another parent available. It's good to be able to discuss the kids with your ex. Your friends don't want to hear you go on about how smart your kids are or what a pain in the ass they are. So it's more than just having more free time as a joint parent. It's also about being able to share feelings with your ex. I'm not in great financial shape, and you ease the burden by bringing them there rather than to daycare. Also I'm busy. I had a meeting really late last night, and I could leave them right there—with someone who really cares about them. (Joint mother A, doctoral student, children are six and twelve, split week.)

A father who had maintained joint custody with his ex-wife for seven years explained:

> It has all the advantages in the world. I have a full sense of participating in their growth. During the bad times for one of us parents, when we had lost a lover or something, the other person picked up the responsibility and spent more time with the kids. (Joint father D, professor, daughters are twelve and fourteen, split week.)

What these joint parents were saying is that joint custody most closely approximates the intact home in that children have full relationships with both parents and parents can count on each other for sharing the labor. Some parents insisted, moreover, that joint custody had advantages beyond those of the intact family:

> I think that children benefit from all the love and stimulation and support the world can provide them. Joint custody really provides them with two homes and two families. They have stayed close to my ex's relatives and have also become attached to my present wife's family. We didn't plan it this way, but joint custody has resulted in something like the traditional extended family for them. (Joint father C, accountant, daughters are nine and ten, split day.)

Another father was quite eloquent on this issue. Here are his thoughts on the superiority of joint custody for his children:

> They have now the advantages of two support systems that are very different; each has a different parent with different strengths and weaknesses, different friends, and a different living space. There are advantages to both places. Their mother lives in a house; this is an apartment. There they have their own room; here they share two rooms. I have tried consciously to make life different here. They sleep Japanese-style in sleeping bags on the floor here, and they love it. This is better than having two things that are kinda like each other so you could say one is nicer.

This father went on to describe the advantages for *himself* of joint custody over marriage:

> It works out remarkably. It's a lot better to have 100 percent of the responsibility 50 percent of the time than 50 percent of the responsibility 100 percent of the time. I can organize my life, responsible only for myself, three to four days a week. This is the best thing that has happened to my life. My relationship with my kids is better. I have this one-to-one relationship with them in a very positive environment—instead of in the deteriorating marriage which was polluting it. . . . Joint custody means being free and a parent at the same time. I don't recommend you need a divorce to do this. There must be some way of reorganizing parenting in the normal situation. (Joint father A, physicist, split week.)

The Disadvantages of Joint Custody. The two major disadvantages of joint custody were: (1) the logistical problems of moving children back and forth between households and (2) the fact that the divorced parents remain tied to each other.

The most vivid description of the logistical problems is this mother's account:

> It's always, "Where are the shoes and the raincoats? All the coats somehow end up there, and I run around screaming "goddamit" and dredge up a hand-me-down of his brother's. It makes mornings hectic. As it is, we each buy each kid a pair of socks a week. They should have fifty-two pairs. I think they eat them or hide them under rocks. Yes, we have to negotiate other things too, like schools. But a major decision comes up every two years. Socks come up every week. (Joint mother A, doctoral student, children are six and twelve, split week.)

More serious are the problems of feeling tied to the ex-spouse. Here are some examples:

> He won't let me leave Cleveland, and I can't get a job here because I'm an art curator and need to be in a city with lots of museums. I have managed to put together several part-time jobs over the past two years, some of which were stimulating and others of which were not. I interviewed for a great job in the East last fall. My idea was for each of us to have one kid and fly the other one back and forth between us. He wouldn't hear of it. If I had full custody I could just lay down the law about that. Joint custody is a complete failure on that issue. (Joint mother B, art historian, children are five and nine, split week.)

Another mother admitted:

> Joint custody does keep people from moving on in life as they would. You don't make as clean a break away from your ex-spouse because you're dealing with him about the children more than a single-custody person deals with the visiting parent. You can't just take off with your kids and start your life over in a new city with no trace of your former life and no ghosts. . . . I would have moved away and gone back to school. Instead, I stayed in town so that we could coparent and postponed going to school until the kids go to college. It is a sacrifice I do not regret and that I would do again, but it is a sacrifice. (Joint mother G, occupational therapist, children are eleven and fifteen, "unstructured".)

A joint father spoke of the disadvantage of having his ex so close that he would bump into her in the grocery store. Here are his words:

> I'm tied to my ex. She lives two blocks away. We arranged the houses to be close in order for the kids to be able to ride their bikes between us, and to

minimize the hassles of switching. There were times I just didn't want to see her, or she me. Sometimes she would pin nasty notes to their clothes. I guess because we *had* to communicate with each other, we learned to do so. We are through the bitterness now. Things have stabilized, and we are both dating often. We are at the point that we can sit and have coffee together now. (Joint father B, college administrator, children are five and nine, split week.)

The comments of these parents raise an extremely important question about joint custody—that is, whether or not it allows interparental conflict to continue. As discussed in the introduction, this issue of conflict has been one of the principal arguments maintained by the courts to dissuade parents from shared custody. It is reinforced by recent evidence that it is parental conflict and not parental absence that places children most at risk for psychological dysfunction.

Despite allusions to conflict in earlier quotes from joint parents, there is no reason to believe that joint custody, as represented in these eleven cases, fosters parental conflict. Parents' ratings of their own post divorce conflict were independent of custody. That is, joint parents reported no more post-divorce conflict than single-custody parents. Furthermore, whereas child adjustment (on parents' ratings and on the Piers-Harris) *was* affected by parental conflict, it was not affected by custody type.

One might argue that only parents who were relatively amicable to begin with would attempt joint custody. This does not seem to be the case here. There was no difference between the predivorce conflict levels of joint- and single-custody families.

Joint parents cited the necessity of continued contact as a disadvantage, but it appears that they somehow managed to negotiate issues about children. All the joint parents (except those labeled as problematic, that is, X, Y, and Z) had a desire to share parenting that superseded the desire to flee from, or fight with, their ex-spouse. One mother put it this way.

The need to communicate with the ex-spouse is a difficulty. You can't cherish your anger. You have to continue to work things out with him, so you have to continue to confront the part of yourself that made the marriage not work. I couldn't have done it without the support of our friends— especially his sister who mediated the negotiations. . . . When you think of the alternative to joint custody, however, it makes this difficulty seem small. (Joint mother D, nurse, daughters are twelve and fourteen, split week.)

Recall that the other main objections to joint custody concern the children's feelings of security in two households and the possibilities for closeness with their parents in the face of the shuttling between them. These questions are addressed through the children's own comments.

Children's Feelings about Joint Custody. Nearly all of the twenty-five joint children were content with the arrangement as it stood. These children echoed the single-custody children in responding to the question, "With whom would you have wanted to live after the divorce?" by saying, "With both!" Here is the statement of a girl who has lived with joint custody for seven years—half of her life:

> I was *worried* when they told us about the divorce. I was seven then, and I had only one friend whose parents were divorced, and her father lived in California. I thought that that was what divorce meant and that I would never see my father. Then they told us we'd be spending our time in both houses—that really neither parent was going away from us. (Girl, fourteen, joint family D.)

The critics of joint custody argue that it deprives children of a sense of security and stability—that all children need one home, one custodian. The children in this study were asked how they felt about living in two houses. Only two children (8 percent) could identify something in their living arrangement that was confusing. Here are their comments:

> Like when I was four or three, I used to bring my blanket over here—my favorite blanket. But I'd have to leave it here because I couldn't bring it to school. After school I go to my mother's house—and I don't have my blanket! But now I'm six and I don't bring it everywhere I go. (Boy, six, joint family A, split week.)

More worrisome are the comments of this little girl:

> It is confusing. Suppose I ask Mom to go skating, and she says yes, and then I tell Dad, and he says "Your friend is sleeping over tonite," and it makes me feel disappointed. Also—whenever my mother lets me have cookies, my dad yells at me for not telling Ma no. But I only do it once in a while so I feel I'm not doing anything wrong. He feels you'll live longer if you eat certain things. She says, "Enjoy life while you have it." I'm in the middle. (Girl, nine, joint family C, split day.)

This girl seems indeed to have some joint-related problems. Both of her parents mentioned the difference in eating habits in the two houses, but they played down the conflict it caused. Presumably, she would not be in the middle of this conflict if she were in the sole custody of one parent and rarely saw the other (cf. Goldstein, Freud, and Solnit). I asked her about this:

> **I:** Do you ever think it would be better just to live with one of them? Then you wouldn't have to worry about two houses and two sets of rules?
> **C:** No, that would be worse. I love them both and would miss them too much. (Girl, nine, joint family C, split day.)

Not only were most joint children not confused, but three-quarters were able to cite advantages to the two-household lifestyle. They described their arrangements as "more fun," "more interesting" or "more confortable," Here are their own words:

> You have access to different things. I have two best friends near my father's house, and school is just across the street. I can walk. My mother lives near Shaker Square—and there must be 10,000 things you can do there. Plus it's nicer in both houses, 'cause you don't have people fighting all the time. (Boy, twelve, joint family A, split week.)

A much younger child made a similar statement:

> See—my daddy lives in the country, and the country has, you know—regular houses and cows and dogs and things. Mommy lives in the city that's got apartments, and you go to restaurants and you can't have no dogs. I like 'em both—the city and the country. (Girl, seven, joint family X, split week.)

Here is a comment from the child who had had the most experience with joint custody:

> I have enjoyed going back and forth. I don't remember any confusion about it, no. And yes, I feel I spend enough time with each parent. I do like to base myself in one house, though, so I don't forget things for school. My father was moving around a lot in town so I chose this house. The houses were always close to each other so I never had a problem getting from one to the other. I prefer this house because most of my stuff is here, and there is more junk food and the TV works better. But if my mother moves to the west side, I will base myself at my father's house in order to stay in the neighborhood. (Girl, fourteen, joint family C, split week.)

I asked the joint children if they felt the need to see one of their parents more than they did. Eight of the twenty-five said yes. Five of these children came from one family. At the time of the interview, they were based with their father in the country and spent alternate weekends with their mother. (Their mother discovered early on that she could not have all five of them in her little apartment every weekend. Thus three of them go to see her one weekend, and two go the next). Here is a comment from the seven-year-old:

> I: What would you have done if they had asked you where you wanted to live?
> C: It would have been hard. I'm glad to live with my dad, but I would like to see Ma more, though. I really wish we could live with both. But you can't split yourself in half and live half with Dad and half with Mom!
> I: What is it you miss most about Mom?

C: She used to read us stories.
I: Doesn't Dad read you stories?
C: Yah, he does. But I like how Mom did it better. (Girl, seven, joint family X.)

This little girl belongs to one of the problematic joint families that will be discussed at the end of this chapter.

How Time Is Spent in Each House

Is "joint custody" just a new term for old-fashioned "visitation"? This is a large question and must be addressed in each chapter as the family functions are described. It is possible, however, to begin to respond to this issue here. Recall that 50 percent of single-custody children reported that time spent with the other parent was either a day of treats or a time to visit friends in the old neighborhood. However, when joint children were asked, "What do you do when you're with the other parent?" they shrugged quizically and listed the same daily activities performed in the house we were in, for example, "I go to school, come home, eat dinner, and ride my bike." Furthermore, just as joint parents had reported that their relationships with their children had improved after the divorce, so did joint children:

> In some ways, it is better to live this way than to be living together. My relationship with both my parents is better than before. I can talk with them separately instead of dealing with them at the same time. I don't like them as much together. They're totally different people, and I like each of them for what they are. And they can be theirselves when they're alone. (Boy, fifteen, joint family G, "unstructured.")

There would seem to be some suggestion from these data that joint custody has more advantages and fewer disadvantages than sole custody. But what about the problematic joint cases? These three families (X, Y, and Z) will be described next with an explanation of: (1) how parents had originally settled on the joint award; (2) what the problems seem to be with the present arrangement; and (3) how the children have adjusted.

The Problematic Joint-Custody Families

Family X

This is the case of a mother who divorced her husband and left their rural home to pursue a career in the city. She had felt stifled to the point of suicidal depression by her life as a homemaker. She needed "space and silence" and therefore left her five children to be based with their father. Her ex said he would not allow her to have full custody of them. She, however, felt too guilty to relinquish custody and become the visitor, although she believes he is a competent parent. Thus the adults decided on joint custody. The children live with their father and travel thirty-five miles to spend alternate weekends with their mother. (The girls go one weekend and the boys the next.) The distance between the two houses, makes the more continuous flowing of children between houses, as in other cases, impossible. Consequently, although the adults are reasonably satisfied with the arrangement—in that neither is inclined to change it—all of the children are unhappy. Each lamented that they missed their mother and that they had cried for months after she left. Each explained that it was not a matter of disliking life with Dad, but that they simply did not see Mom enough. They have made their needs known, and the mother is fully aware that they want more time from her. She feels guilty but maintains that she still needs time alone and that she cannot give them more time now. The situation could change in one of two ways with time. The children may grow accustomed to seeing her seldom, or she may agree to increase their time with her, as she begins to feel more "together."

In terms of the children's adjustment, using the standard measures—none of the five children scored a low self-concept on the Piers-Harris. The mother reported that one of the boys had dropped a grade since the divorce. Another boy, on the other hand, had gone up a grade since the divorce. It is not clear—even though the children say they are sad and disappointed, whether or not these children are being damaged by this situation. Their mother is sanguine. She feels they have shown great resiliency. None of them has shown signs of depression except that when they talk about custody, they still cry. They have several factors in their favor: (1) Their parents are no longer in conflict; (2) each parent believes the other is competent; (3) money is not a dire problem; (4) they have additional support from both grandmothers. Whether or not they will be emotionally scarred from having lost some contact with their mother at a young age is an empirical question.

Family Y

This is a family of particular interest because the parents were court-ordered, against their wishes, to practice joint custody. Both parents, claiming the other unfit, had fought for sole custody of their daughters, ages eleven and twelve. The mother's lawyer explained to me that the judge had considered this a difficult case. He felt that neither parent alone was competent to rear children, and yet foster placement was not quite warranted.

The judge viewed Mrs. Y as a potentially violent person (she had made homicidal threats to her in-laws and had abused her daughter), but she was also a loving and affectionate mother. The judge saw Mr. Y as a "dry" personality who seemed to show little emotion and certainly no positive emotion. Mr. Y, however, seemed more stable than his ex-wife and also lived near his own mother who could help out with the children. The judge awarded joint custody. This, he hoped, would allow the girls the physical security of their father's care, while still permitting them access to their mother's love.

This was classified as a problematic case because both parents are extremely unhappy about the joint award and try to undermine each other. Mr. Y says his ex-wife is "filthy" and "insane." Mrs. Y says her ex-husband is "a liar, immature, and capable of no love." At first blush, this case appears to be the materialization of the nightmare joint-custody critics have prophesized. Indeed, the Y parents bring to mind those dueling parents of Henry James's *What Maisie Knew*, who, to their great chagrin, were awarded joint custody of their young daughter. In the case of Maisie's parents, as with Mr. and Mrs. Y, it appeared that:

> husband and wife alike had been crippled by the heavy hand of justice, which, in the last resort met on neither side their indignant claim to get, as they called it, everything. If each was only to get half this seemed to concede that neither was so base as the other pretended, or, to put it differently, offered them both as bad indeed, since they were only as good as each other. . . . They girded their loins, they felt as if the quarrel had only begun. They felt indeed more married than ever. . . .[2]

At the time of the interview, Mr. Y was still trying to prevent Mrs. Y from seeing the girls. He is able to do this because she is poor. She has no car and so must pay for the girls' bus trip to her home, thirty-five miles away, and for her own fare as well, because he will not allow them to get on the bus unescorted. This is why she only sees the girls every other week. Mrs. Y would love to take him to court but cannot afford it.

The girls report, "Our mother and father hate each other's guts. They still fight every chance they get." The girls were asked if, for this reason, they would prefer to be in the custody of one parent and rarely or never see the other. They would not. They are content with the present arrangement. They deplore the continued fighting but note that it has decreased enormously since the divorce since the parents simply do not get as many chances to fight.

It was interesting to note that both the mother's violence and her tenderness (as perceived by the judge) were manifest in the interview. During the three hours that I was asking questions, mother and daughters never stopped bickering. Mrs. Y can speak to them in a very harsh way. Surprisingly, their family TAT reflected more warmth and support than almost any other in the sample. The three sat closely together and collaborated happily in their stories. Mrs. Y spoke in gentle and sincere tones, and the girls did not fight with each other.

There is some clear maladjustment in the daughters. Although their Pier-Harris scores (51 and 55) are below the sample mean (60), each is above the cut-off score for low self-concept (46). According to the parental ratings, however, there are some behavior problems, especially in the twelve-year-old girl. Sally dropped three grades since the divorce. Her lying and "bitchiness" have become a problem. Mrs. Y felt that both grls have low self-esteem, and she described both as "compulsive eaters." Both gained a great deal of weight around the time of the divorce.

The origin of these children's problems is patent. They were both un-wanted at birth (according to mother) and have lived through a childhood of violence. The difficult task at this point is to understand what if anything would improve their situation. The literature reviewed in chapter 1 would point toward single custody in this case because parental conflict is a very serious stressor. The girls do not want this, however. In any case, it would be difficult to choose between these marginally competent parents. (This was the judge's dilemma.)

Because this is a perplexing case that epitomizes some of the problems of joint custody, I have asked several clinicians to comment on it during the past year. When asked what the best alternative for these children would be, Braulio Montalvo, a therapist at the Philadelphia Child Guidance Clinic who has been critical of joint custody, concluded, "They should remain in joint custody and spend ten hours per week at the Newman Center!" Indeed, it will probably be the presence or absence of extrafamilial support that determines the psychological outcome for these children.

Family Z

Both Mr. and Mrs. Z argued originally for full custody, claiming the other unfit. Mrs. Z, desiring to avoid the trauma of a custody battle in court, finally agreed both to joint custody and to relinquishing the family home. At the time of the interview, the children were living with her during the week and with their father on weekends.

The children are content with the arrangement; there is nothing about it they would change. Mr. Z is delighted with the arrangement. He explained that his relationships with all the children had improved, and that he and his wife had worked out a civil and flexible arrangement.

The interview with Mrs. Z produced a very different picture. She feels joint custody is the worst thing that ever happened to her. She feels very much victimized by the fact that she was "forced" to give up both custody and her share of the house in order to protect the children from a custody battle. Now she is living in a housing project, which is apparently a major embarrassment to her and the children. Her ex has remained alone in their house. Mrs. Z says that the word *joint* really means nothing because she still feels totally responsible for the children. She does not want her ex to take more responsibility for them, however, because she sees him as a violent and insensitive person. If not for joint custody, she would move out of the area with the children and "begin life again."

The children do not want to move, however; they are comfortable with the amount of time spent in both houses. None of them showed a depressed Piers-Harris score. The parents' ratings indicated that the nine-year-old son was having problems with aggressiveness and tantrums. He has been diagnosed as hypoglycemic, and the relationship between this condition and his acting out is unclear. Both parents and his teacher have reported that when he avoids food that aggravate the hypoglycemia, his behavior is "100 percent improved."

Conclusions

The two important findings of this chapter concern (1) the consultation of children in matters of custody and (2) the advantages and disadvantages of the three custody options from the families' points of view.

Lee Salk's position on consulting children about custody is that, although their opinions should be elicited, children must be assured that the burden of the final choice rests not on them but on the adults. The children in this study who were consulted had not been reassured about the limits of their choice. Consequently, they agonized over having to hurt one of their parents. Of particular interest was the fact that parents were unaware of how their children had suffered over the choice. Other studies as well have found that at the time of divorce, adults are so engrossed in their own pain that they are nearly oblivious to the needs of their children. Kelly and Wallerstein (1976), for example, reported that 85 percent of their sample had failed to tell children anything about the divorce, leaving them to find out about it via the newspaper or the taunts of neighbors' children. This problem itself points toward the wisdom of short-term counseling services for divorcing families—in order to provide some extra support for all members and to provide children with a neutral context in which to ask questions and express feelings about the divorce. One such counseling project was established by Judith Wallerstein and Joan Kelly in Marin County, California. Another was established by Marla Isaacs at the Philadelphia Child Guidance Clinic.

In terms of comparing the virtues of single-parent and joint custody, this chapter has produced several findings that merit further investigation. It is essential to bear in mind that this is an exploratory study, based on a self-selected sample. We cannot conclude on the basis of these findings that joint custody always works effectively or even that it works effectively eight out of eleven times. Nonetheless, these findings challenge the categorical statements of those who believe that joint custody can never work. With this caveat in mind, we can review the findings of this chapter.

1. Contrary to the warnings of many judges, there was no evidence that the joint custody families in this study sustained more post-divorce conflict than single-parent custody.
2. Contrary to the warnings of Goldstein, Freud, and Solnit (1973), there was no evidence that children experienced a great disruption from living in two houses. In fact, most children felt their new lifestyle held certain advantages over the nuclear-family household.
3. Whereas many single parents had "split the scene," forfeiting all contact with the children, no joint parent had done so.
4. Aproximately half the children in single custody desired more contact with their noncustodial parent.
5. No joint father had ceased to support the children financially, as many noncustodial fathers had.
6. There was some evidence in the sample that joint children had maintained meaningful relationships with both parents, in contrast with the single-custody children for whom the "visit" was a vacation.
7. Single-custody parents reported feeling "burned out" and "overwhelmed" in a way that joint parents did not.

Points 6 and 7 form the essence of the argument that joint custody should be the presumption of law. Joint custody has some disadvantages, however, that should not be ignored. One major disadvantage of joint over single custody was being tied to the ex-spouse. Some single-custody parents in the sample had left town after the divorce in order to start life over in a new environment without painful associations from the past. This can be a good coping strategy. It makes people feel adventuresome and hopeful about the future. Joint parents were not able to do this, and it was painful for some. [We should not overlook the fact that two joint families (18 percent) were able to continue joint custody long distance by splitting the years, or alternating years, but the fact remains that joint custody is more feasible where parents live near each other.]

One family who declined to participate in the study involved a father who wanted split-week joint custody and a mother who desired to take their young sons back to Israel with her. If joint custody were mandatory, it is very difficult to imagine what would happen in such cases.

It is easier to speculate on what made some joint families so happy than it is to pinpoint why a given joint case was unsuccessful. In families X, Y, and Z, the discontent was overdetermined. In X and Y, the parents lived thirty-five miles apart. Mothers Y and Z were on welfare, as were none of the other joint families. This contributed to the raging resentment toward the ex-spouse that is not auspicious for joint parenting. The Z children have had psychosomatic problems for years, which had only complicated the typical problems of parental negotiations. Family Y is unique in the study in that the parents seem to have glaring psychopathic tendencies. Possibly the most important factor is that Y and Z felt forced into joint custody, and X is still ambivalent about the decision. One can only hope that the children in these three families will show the resiliency of James's Maisie, who survives despite her parents' cruel games.

In conclusion, the results of this chapter seem to suggest that joint custody in the successful cases has more advantages and fewer disadvantages than sole custody, but this suggestion must be followed through each of the chapters on family functions.

Notes

1. D. Ehrensaft, "When Women and Men Mother," *Socialist Review* 49 (1980):37-73.
2. H. James, *What Maisie Knew* (New York: Penguin Books, 1979), p. 19.

3 Economics

Income Data

The purpose of this chapter is to explore the economic problems and advantages of being a single mother, father, or joint parent. As predicted, money-related problems were much more serious for mothers than for fathers. On the Rank-Stress scale, mothers rated money as most stressful—number 1 out of nine items—whereas fathers rated it number 3. Table 3-1 shows income figures that explain this difference clearly. The median income for women dropped as much as two brackets whereas the men's median income increased or stayed the same after divorce. Many women's working incomes were augmented by alimony or child support. Note, however, that the mothers' incomes reported in table 3-1 *include* any such supplement.

These findings are consistent with government statistics on postdivorce income. According to the U.S. Bureau of the Census (1977), the mean income of divorced women with children was $9,608—or 53 percent of the mean income of intact famlies—$18,206. Why do women's incomes plunge so drastically after divorce? The answer is *not* that women elect to stay home and live on welfare. In this study, only three women (12 percent) were not working outside the home at the time of the interview. (One had a physical disability, one could not afford to pay for child care out of her salary, and the other simply preferred to stay home with the children.) The remaining 88 percent of the sample was gainfully employed. This statistic is very close to the national statistic: 82 percent of divorced mothers with school-age children work outside the home (U.S. Bureau of Labor Statistics 1978).

The reason most women are poorer than men after divorce is that men earn more money. In 1979 women earned 59 percent of what men earned. This is not because men had more education. In 1979 a woman with a college degree earned $1,000 per year less than a man with an eighth grade education.[1] One illustration of this disparity in this study was a father with a high school diploma working as a toolmaker and earning an income in the $20,000-$25,000 bracket, whereas a mother with a B.A. working as a nurse fell one bracket below him. Her income fell in the same bracket as the father with a ninth-grade education working as a forklift operator.

Table 3-1
Median Income for Men and Women before and after Divorce

	Time	
Custody	Predivorce	Postdivorce
Highly educated mothers	$22,500	$14,500
Highly educated fathers	17,000	19,500
Mothers with low education	17,000	6,500
Fathers with low education	17,000	17,000
Joint mothers	17,000	6,500
Joint fathers	17,000	17,000

It was somewhat surprising that men's incomes did not drop after divorce since many were paying child support to their ex-wives. The reason was that many men had been promoted or had had salary increases since the divorce that offset those expenses either partially or completely. This income stability is reflected in their responses to two questions about their felt economic stress.

Parents were asked, "Is money a major worry in your life?" They responded on a 1-5 scale, indicating never, rarely, sometimes, often, or always. Their answers showed that women worry about money significantly more after divorce than before it (see table 3-2). Men, on the other hand, worry less about money after divorce than before it.

Participants were interviewed about the sources of their financial stress after divorce. These sources included alimony and child support, finding and changing jobs, managing money, and obtaining credit. The discussion begins with a consideration of single-custody mothers and fathers. (Again,

Table 3-2
Parents' Ratings of How Much They Worry about Money

	Mothers[a]			Fathers[b]		
	High Education	Low Education	Joint	High Education	Low Education	Joint
n	8	8	9	8	8	9
Time						
Predivorce	2.0	3.0	2.44	3.5	3.5	3.33
Postdivorce	3.87	4.25	3.44	2.62	2.62	3.0

Note: Higher numbers indicate higher stress.
[a] Women worry more often after divorce than before it [t(48) = 2.01; $p < .05$].
[b] Men worry less about money after divorce than before [t(48) = 2.13; $p < .05$].

because joint custody involves some unique issues, the joint families will be discussed separately at the end of the chapter.)

Alimony and Child Support

Single-Custody Mothers

All the single-custody mothers except one had been awarded child support by the court. Half of all mothers were awarded alimony as well. (Among those who did not receive alimony, half had waived it, and half had fought unsuccessfully for it.)

Only half of the mothers reported that their ex-husbands supported them reliably. The others had major problems collecting support. Some representative comments follow:

> At first he was paying reliably, but then he started slipping, so I took him to court, and now his checks come regularly. The amount, however, is not fair because it only covers child care—not clothes, rent, and amenities. (Professor, daughter is seven.)

A mother who had lived an upper-middle-class lifestyle said:

> My son has massive medical bills because of a variety of problems he has had since birth. The judge said his father was responsible for the bills "as long as he is able"—which left it wide open. Although he is a wealthy man, he has paid none of those bills. Luckily, we went on medicaid. (Secretary, son is four.)

A third mother said:

> The settlement was completely unfair! I got no alimony, and he got the house too. My second lawyer told me I was really taken. He got me $45 per week child support—for four kids!—but my ex never paid it. I got notification later that he was filing for bankruptcy, and that as long as I was working, I was responsible for them. (Nurse's aid, children are eight, ten, and sixteen and living at home.)

The other half of the single mothers claimed that their ex had never missed a payment. One sympathetic mother commented, "Unfortunately, it's a lot of money for him to pay out, but not very much for us to live on."

Although many women were clearly still angry about the financial settlement, most were resigned to the situation. Their position was that it was not worth the grief and the expense to continue fighting for more money.

I was impressed by the fact that several women were unable to explain their financial settlement to me during the interview. They admitted that they were confused about what they had signed and about how some of the decisions had been made. Many women reported that their lawyers had not been helpful. Some women even felt they had been cheated by signing things unwittingly. Seven of the sixteen single-custody mothers felt that their lawyers had served them incompetently. Here is a typical comment:

> I went to my lawyer in January 1976, and he has done nothng about the fact that my ex has never made a single child-support payment. They have all assured me that he does have to pay, but nothing gets done. They don't return phone calls or even answer my letters. It makes you feel like you're invisible—that there is nothing you can do to make the law work for you. (Store manager, son is fifteen.)

The importance of seeing a second lawyer arose in several cases:

> My first lawyer was just horrible. I was getting absolutely nothing. The day I was supposed to close on the house, I decided to call another lawyer. He read through the papers and asked me if I had been caught in adultery because he had never seen such a terrible settlement. I was getting $750 out of a property worth $14,000. He had forged my name on a mortgage, and the first lawyer refused to fight for me. (Teacher's aid, son is fifteen.)

Six of the seven mothers who felt their lawyers were unsatisfactory were mothers in the low-education group—with low incomes. A number of authors (for example, Weiss 1973) have discussed the treatment that low-income people receive at the hands of professionals and social-service agencies. In contrast to the mothers' experiences with lawyers, all the single fathers reported that their lawyers had done at least an adequate job. One of the fathers is a lawyer himself, and five others (31 percent) had called upon a lawyer who was either a brother or a friend. Clearly, professional men are more likely than homemakers to have friends who are lawyers. Even the father with a ninth-grade education had a lawyer who was a friend; they belonged to the same rifle club. Whether or not lawyers are less respectful to women, or particularly to low-income women, it is clear that the isolated predivorce lives of many of these women put them at a disadvantage in choosing a lawyer. (Women's pre-divorce isolation is pursued in chapter 5.)

Single-Custody Fathers and Alimony

Six of the sixteen fathers were paying either alimony or support for a child in the mother's custody. All six felt that obligation to be unfair. Their comments ran as follows:

I am paying child support for my daughter, and it's an unfair amount. I'm paying my ex as much now as when she was employed. I'm afraid my ex is benefiting from that money, and I don't want that. I would be glad to put the same amount of money aside in a college trust fund for the kids—but she won't hear of that. (Physician, son is thirteen.)

Said another father:

I agreed to pay her alimony for two years. This is unfair. She has done nothing to deserve this; she can work. But I couldn't fight it because I wanted custody. All along she wanted me to have custody, but her lawyer told her to use custody as a bargaining chip to get all the money she could. (Business executive, daughter is six.)

With six fathers partially supporting their ex-wives, it seems incongruous that their perceived financial stress could be less than it was before the divorce. The questions about work help to explain this matter.

Work

The Fathers

Participants were asked if they had changed jobs, salary, or working hours after the divorce. Whereas the mothers underwent major changes in their working conditions, the fathers underwent relatively few changes. Forty-four percent of the fathers said that they were making more money after the divorce than before because of pay raises and promotions. In contrast to the mothers, none of the fathers said he was working longer hours than before the divorce, and 56 percent of the fathers actually said they were working shorter hours in order to stay home with the children. Some sample comments follow:

My colleagues at work have known Josh since he was a baby. They gave me a shower when he was born. They are terrifically understanding when I need to leave early or arrive later because he is sick or something. (Professor, son is seven.)

Said another father:

Yes, I work shorter hours to be home with Greg more. This doesn't affect my income—it just puts me on a tighter schedule. But my values have changed, and I feel good about working a little less. (Physician, son is thirteen.)

And finally:

> I definitely work shorter hours. I am in charge of the company now. I can take off lunch hours to spend with her. My time is really my own. (Business executive, daughter is seven.)

Only one father had moved into a less desirable working/financial situation after the divorce. His account suggests that although men generally fare better than women economically, child custody will be more of a burden for the blue-collar man than for the professional man:

> Before the divorce I had a good mechanic's job. It paid great, but the hours was irregular. I'd be on one shift one day and another shift on Tuesday. It was impossible to schedule sitters. So I changed jobs and took a cut in pay of $100 a week. I work an extra eight hours a week for the same amount of money. And now I have sitters to pay. The new job is more tedious, too— just fixing tires, and they're all the same. I hate it. But with four little girls—what are you going to do? (Mechanic, daughters are four, eight, twelve, and fourteen.)

Regular yet flexible hours are features usually associated with elite jobs. Note that the men quoted here who spoke of flexible hours are professionals.

The Mothers

Nine of the thirteen mothers who worked outside the home had never held a full-time job prior to the divorce and were forced to go out for financial reasons. Here are some of their accounts:

> When he left, I had to do something to support these seven kids. I had no skills and could not afford to go to school so I watched the children of working mothers in my home for a year. I nearly went crazy spending my days and nights with no one but young, demanding children. I had to get out of the house, and my friend offered me a job in her printing house. I couldn't afford daycare, so I took my youngest to work with me, and she would play on the floor while I worked. That worked out well, but when it came time for her to go to first grade, she wouldn't. She was used to being with me constantly and screamed and clung desperately when I took her to school. This lasted through her entire first grade. By second grade, she was OK. (High school teacher, children are eleven, fourteen, fifteen, and seventeen, living at home.)

Several mothers really felt terrified about leaving the home and entering the marketplace:

I had not worked in twenty years of marriage. He didn't want me to. Now I'd prefer not to. I'm scared to death to be out there—but I have no choice because of the money situation. Now at my age, with no training, I have to go out and compete for a job with young girls. Besides, I figured out that in clothes and transportation, it costs almost as much as I could make in a week. So I just started with Avon, so if a kid is sick I could stay at home. I dislike doing it; you feel so pushy. And you don't make that much money. (Avon representative, children are ten, fifteen, and sixteen.)

A few mothers felt guilty about having to leave their children, who were already distressed about the separation, in order to go to work:

I had to go to work. I didn't want to. I felt terrible about leaving the kids; they were going through so many changes after the divorce. I wanted to stay with them. I had to take Amy to her teacher screaming and I would leave her there and could hear her screaming until I left the building. What could I do? We had no money and I had to feed them. (Currently unemployed mother, children are six and nine.)

In addition to the problems of women who had never worked are the problems of women who had to change jobs or hours after the divorce:

I preferred secretarial work, but it didn't pay enough for me to survive, so I had to take a managerial job at Magic-Mart. The hours are brutal. It's eight to six on the short days and eight to ten on long days. I get so tired, and then I bitch and take it out on everyone. For a while I threw myself into it and never went out. I wasn't a person. I even thought I'd be risking my standing with the company if I had an affair. So I stayed home. After I became ill and needed surgery, I realized I had to live a little and couldn't let Magic-Mart rule my life. (Store manager, son is fifteen.)

Said another mother:

After the divorce I began working nights so I could work all night and spend days with the kids. The disadvantage? When you don't have any sleep, you're not very nice to people. It has dulled my memory too. I would prefer days, but I can't just now. (LPN, children are four and eight.)

Managing Money

Single-Custody Mothers

In addition to working, budgeting money for the family was new for many women. Among the women in the high-education group, 75 percent had not managed the family budget during the marriage. This was a surprising finding since this group includes several professionals. Actually, more of the

women with low education—50 percent—had been responsible for budgeting than the high-education women. Lilian Rubin, who found that more
working-class women than middle-class women were in control of the family
budget, articulated this rule: When there is money left over after bills are
paid, you will find men in control of money. Where there are no decisions
to be made about the money because it all goes for necessities, you will find
women in control of it. In fact, women in this sample who reported that it
had always been their job to pay the bills came from homes that were always
in financial turmoil. Their comments are consistent with Rubin's rule:

> I took care of the bills as best I could during the marriage. It was borrowing
> Peter to pay Paul. He would never handle it. When a collection agency
> would call, he would hand the phone to me. So I was used to managing
> money—and believe me, it's a lot easier now than when he was around.
> (Unemployed mother, daughters are thirteen and fourteen.)

An example of the *middle*-class homemaker who had *not* been in control of
money is this mother:

> I had never handled money. I was never allowed to write a check when we
> were married. The lawyer asked how much I needed to run a house on, and
> I had no idea. I found out after all was settled that he made $19,000 and I
> almost died. I never would have agreed to $135 a week had I known that.
> (Avon representative, children are ten, fifteen, and sixteen.)

The apprehension about dealing with financial matters is best exemplified
by this woman:

> I didn't even know how much money he made. Money was "none of my
> business." He just gave it to me. I had never had to worry about balancing an
> account. For the past four years I have paid everything by money order to
> avoid balancing a checkbook, but that got too expensive. I finally got a
> checkbook two weeks ago. (Nurse's aid, children are eight, ten, and sixteen.)

Single-Custody Fathers

Among the sixteen fathers, only two reported that their wives used to
handle money in the household. They described learning this task as "one
more pain in the neck"—but not as anything difficult.

Moving

It has often been mentioned in the divorce literature that moving in itself is
stressful. Here are the accounts of parents who had to move after the
divorce.

Single-Custody Fathers

Eighty-one percent of the fathers were able to stay in the house they had been living in during the marriage. Those who were forced to move had wives who were remaining in the house with the child who was in her custody. Of the thirteen fathers who stayed, five decided voluntarily to move out, and only three of those for financial reasons. Although in general these numbers do not indicate that moving was a major problem for men, they did report regrets:

> I grew up in that house, in that neighborhood. I love the lake. Love boating. Besides leaving behind the children she got custody of, the move itself was traumatic for me. (Lawyer, sons are twelve and fourteen.)

Single-Custody Mothers

Half of the single-custody mothers had either lost their houses to their ex-husbands or they had been forced to move from their houses for financial reasons. These moves created a variety of problems. Two of the eight women who moved were forced to return to their parents' houses:

> I had no choice but to move back home although I didn't want to. I didn't want to be a daughter again. We get along all right, but I still wish I had my own place. They are doting grandparents and try to stop me from disciplining Danny. It is hard for me to tell them to stop because I am supposed to be grateful for their generosity. Also, my going out revolves around their schedule because I need them to babysit. Not to mention the little things of not having privacy and not being able to rearrange the furniture. (Secretary, son is four.)

Every clinician who works with families will recognize the scenario just described. The divorced mother who moves back to her family of origin has a very difficult time maintaining the executive role vis-à-vis her own child. The task of the therapist in such situations is to support the mother in her parental role and demonstrate to the grandparents the importance of not confusing the child with two imperatives. Very often the treatment plan includes encouraging the mother to move out as soon as she is financially able.

Another problem that comes with moving is discrimination against the divorced mother. One-third of the mothers reported difficulty finding an apartment for this reason:

> I had a terrible time finding an apartment. One landlord said he had had bad experiences with divorced women—that they go back to their husbands—and

others assumed you lived a swinging-singles life. I heard it from more than
one landlord. I was beginning to think I'd live anywhere. I protested the
first couple of times, but it was clear it wasn't penetrating. (Assistant professor, daughter is seven.)

Other mothers were told that women could not do the necessary maintenance on the apartment:

I had actually rented an apartment with a big security deposit when I got a
phone call from the woman saying her husband said no way was he renting
to a divorcced mother with two children. I raised hell with him, and he said,
"Who will cut the lawn and change the washers?" I said—if a woman
needs to do those things, she will. (Unemployed mother, daughters are thirteen and fourteen.)

One mother was in the process of being evicted at the time of the interview.
Her landlord told her that her children would not be so noisy if they had a
father. In fact, several mothers, when looking for apartments, were given
lectures on the effects of father absence:

One landlord said to me, "Children run wild without a father in the home.
They don't listen to their mothers as much, and then they grow up and get
into all kinds of trouble and drugs." It was absolutely humiliating to have
to listen to this crap from total strangers. (Unemployed mother, children
are six and nine.)

The attitude of these women toward the housing discrimination was
somewhat resigned. They felt that it was foolish to try and force a man to
rent to them and then live downstairs from him or have to depend on him
for maintenance. Only one father spoke of this kind of discrimination:

Two places didn't want divorced people with children. One place told me
flat out—"We've had divorced folks with kids, and forget it—we've had
our fill of those people." (Machinist, children are eleven, twelve, and fourteen.)

Credit

The Equal Opportunity in Credit Act of 1975 (Public Law 93-495) prohibits
any creditor from discriminating against any applicant on the basis of sex or
marital status with respect to any aspect of a credit transaction. The law
states that a person with a grievance about such discrimination may file a
suit for actual damages and for punitive damages up to $10,000. Nonethe-
less, a full 50 percent of the mothers (but none of the fathers) reported having trouble getting credit. Here are some of their comments:

> My ex's credit rating is so bad that I still can't get credit—even though I
> make good money and pay my bills. (Student and secretary, children are
> seven, ten, and eleven.)

Another mother who encountered problems with credit was extremely
tenacious and finally won the battle:

> When my girlfriend moved in with us, we had to put all the kids in bunk
> beds, so I went to a store and found them for $350, and they didn't want to
> give me credit. I had had three charge accounts and worked full time and
> had never had any problems. I fought with them every day and finally they
> gave it to me. (Unemployed mother, children are six and nine.)

Another mother had discovered several of the liabilities of being a divorced
woman:

> I had to fight for a Sears card like you wouldn't believe. Then they only
> gave me $100. After that I was turned down by all the others. My counselor
> told me to keep pushing. That's how I finally got the $100. . . . And you
> lose your social security after divorce. Ten years you pay into it—and it's
> gone. All the stocks and bonds were in his name too. I hadn't known that.
> (Avon representative, children are ten, fifteen, and sixteen.)

The mother just quoted was right both about social security and about
stocks. At the time of the interview, a wife was entitled to no retirement,
survivor, or disability benefits if she divorced her husband before twenty
years of marriage. If such a woman did not go to work after the divorce, she
would never collect social security. Even those women who did go out to
work would ultimately collect less, however, because all their years as
homemakers would be considered as no income, which would decrease the
average benefit base. Since the interview, this law has changed from twenty
years to ten years of marriage necessary to ensure the benefits a married
woman would receive. With regard to stock—New York state is one of
forty-three "separate-property" jurisdictions—meaning that a wife has no
legal claim to stocks or property in the ex-husband's name.[2]

Economic Advantages of Single Parenthood

The Mothers

If the women had more problems with money, they also reported more advantages to having the new responsibility. Their responses centered around
the theme of finally feeling that they "owned" their own lives:

Advantages to controlling the money? I feel like a person! When I was young my parents told me how to breathe and how to function, and then I went into a marriage where my husband told me how to breathe and how to function. Really this is the first time I'm a person. I never would have worked otherwise and never would have found out that I have some intelligence and something to contribute to society. (Therapy aid, children are ten and fifteen.)

Several women talked of the exhilaration of being out in the workworld:

Financially we are better off now. There were times when there was no money for food then. I have less money now but more control. I work full time and go to school, but it doesn't feel like a burden. I get a lot of positive feedback from both—that I am capable of something. (Student and secretary, children are seven, ten, and eleven.)

A mother who had gone from a luxurious lifestyle during the marriage to a much simpler existence living with her parents and collecting medicaid had this to say:

We used to eat in exclusive restaurants three times a week, and when I was depressed, I would take my charge accounts and buy designer clothes. Now I don't even own the bed I sleep in, but at least I am a free agent. It's a horrible feeling when you are selling your peace of mind for good clothes. I earn peanuts now, but anything I buy is really mine! (Secretary and student, son is four.)

Another mother talked about the happiness she had found in becoming close with other women in the same situation:

I work nights which is very hard, very exhausting. But on the night shift all the workers are women—either divorced or students—and everyone is loving and sympathetic to each other. It's a very special shift. (LPN, children are four and eight.)

The Fathers

Some fathers did report some advantages to the single managing of home economics:

She was a spendthrift. If there was $200 in the bank she'd go get it and spend it. (Architect, son is four.)

Said another father:

I'm banking money for the first time. I bought some land and a cabin. We're doing a lot of things now—like skiing every weekend. (School principal, children are twelve and fourteen.)

Economics and the Joint-Custody Families

Arrangements

Joint families had a variety of financial arrangements. In the split-week cases, the adults shared the children's expenses according to a formula based on income. This formula in each case necessitated the husband's paying out a monthly sum to his ex-wife.

In approximately half of the joint cases in which the children were based with the fathers, the fathers totally supported the children and paid nothing to their ex-wives. In one case, a mother paid her ex $200 per month for child care. In two cases, the children were based with their mothers. In one of those families, the expenses were shared, with the mother's paying more because she earned more. In the last case, the father paid one-third of his salary to his ex-wife who was on welfare. Table 3-3 shows the financial-support arrangements for the eleven joint families.

Money was the number 1 stressor for joint mothers as it was for single mothers. Joint fathers rated money as number 2 on the Rank-Stress scale. There seems to be a difference, however, in the economic negotiations of single and joint parents. *Fifty-six percent of the single-custody mothers had to return to court because their ex refused to pay child support.* One-third of these women had not been successful at the time of the interview in receiving any money from their ex. In contrast, none of the joint parents had returned to court over money. Although there were serious disagreements over money among joint parents, they were able to negotiate out of court. This is clearly preferable, both in terms of emotional stress and the cost of legal battles.

One exception should be mentioned immediately. In the problematic case of family Y, the mother was not receiving the $40 per week that the

Table 3-3
Financial Arrangements of the Joint Families

	Joint Arrangements		
	Children Split Week (Four Cases)	*Children Based with Father (Five Cases)*	*Children Based with Mother (Two Cases)*
Type of financial arrangement	Parents split expenses by a formula based on earnings (three cases).	Father supports children (four cases).	Formula based on earning; mother pays more (one case).
	Father supports ex, who is a student (one case).	Father gets $200 a month from ex for daycare (one case).	Father supports children with one-third his salary (one case).

court had ordered. Because of her ex-husband's own financial situation, she felt sure that scraping up the money to fight him in court would ultimately be pointless. She is simply resigned to his not paying child support.

The joint families had other financial problems, and they are described below.

Money-Related Problems of Joint Custody

He pays child support based on my income. It's not fair, but it's fair enough. I am earning $170 a week. Last year he made $55,000 and paid $5,000 to his first wife. My income last year was $5,000. He pays the mortgage on this house and taxes and gives me $200 a month for food. Sometime last winter he decided that was too much and stopped paying. I assumed he was paying the bills until they wanted to turn off the electricity. He is both absent-minded and hostile, and they go nicely together. He is paying now. (Doctoral student, children are six and twelve, split week.)

Communication problems about money were not uncommon:

When the children were based with her, she would take them shopping and show me the bill later, and that became a source of conflict. It was something we had to talk through. We decided it was OK for her to buy things for the kids, as long as she mentioned it first and said, "I'm taking Candy for a winter coat." (Professor, children are eleven and fifteen, "unstructured.")

One family was going through a financial struggle at the time of the interview:

Starting next month I'm not paying her anything anymore. We had an agreement that when her income went up, I would stop paying. It was irritating to me to pay her $400 a month and see her take expensive vacations when I had to give up stuff. (College administrator, children are five and nine, split week.)

The ex-wife of the man just quoted was interviewed a month later. This is her account:

He just stopped sending the check suddenly. I was furious. I wrote him a note reminding him of our agreement. . . . He went a check the next day with an apology. We have negotiated it down to $160 a month because I'm earning a bit more now. But I certainly don't earn what he does. (Art historian, children are five and nine, split week.)

Another joint mother had actually changed the living arrangements for the children for financial reasons. She and her ex-husband had always had joint custody, but the children had been based with her. She went bankrupt after the divorce, and her ex refused to give her more money. She then gave him an ultimatum either to pay more or to take the children to live with him. When he unexpectedly chose the latter, she had mixed feelings about their leaving. She was threatened with eviction and so had to make the switch. Both parents and both children now report that it had a positive outcome. The children enjoy being based with their father because it has given them a new closeness with him, without diminishing the closeness with their mother.

A final example of the economic problems faced by joint parents is that of a mother who wanted to leave town to pursue her career but could not. She is the art historian, seeking a curator's job. She felt sure that she could find a position elsewhere, but she is bound to stay in the area to preserve joint custody.

As mentioned previously, one positive feature of joint custody as it is represented in this study is that the financial settlements are less often taken to court. Why should this be the case? Recall that over 50 percent of the single-custody mothers felt that the child support they received was not fair according to what their ex-spouse earned and according to what they needed. Only two of the joint mothers felt that the amount was unfair, and one had "mixed feelings." One of these was the unemployed mother who was not receiving the $40 awarded to her. The other mother said of her situation, "It's not fair, but it's fair enough," alluding to her ex-husband's high income. A third complaint of unfair settlement came from a problematic joint family in which the mother had wanted full custody. She reported:

> I thought we were more in debt than we were, so I gave up the house—just gave it up—didn't even sell my half. I was harassed by him. I gave up everything so there wouldn't be a custody battle. I was living with my parents and had to get out of there. So I settled for peanuts. He should be paying more and has agreed to start doing so. (Joint mother Z, split week.)

These accounts do not appear as extreme as those of the single-custody mothers. Among the three abovementioned cases, one husband was on welfare, one mother felt the amount was "fair enough," and the third said her ex has agreed to pay her more. (Mr. Z also reported that he intended to do this.)

As for the joint fathers—all said they found the settlement fair except for one who felt his wife was living somewhat extravagently because of his supplements and who thus had mixed feelings. (This is joint father B, whose wife was taking expensive vacations.) Another joint father who was totally supporting his ex was unusually sympathetic to her feelings that he was not giving her a "gift." Here are his words:

> I totally support her. I pay for my mortgage and the rent on her apartment and her tuition, food, clothes, and everything for the kids. It doesn't feel

great because I could use a new car and would like a new stereo. But on the other hand, I understand that she invested a lot of time early in our relationship and made it possible for me to go out and work and get seniority and earn the high salary that I do. (Joint father E, split week.)

This again is quite a contrast to the single fathers—all of whom felt they were paying too much. Why should joint parents be more able to negotiate finances out of court and to arrive at settlements that seem fair? One possibility is that couples who were more compatible in the first place would be the ones to opt for joint custody. The datum that mitigates against that interpretation is that joint-custody parents rated their predivorce conflict as high as did single-custody parents. But, unlike the singles, joint parents live near each other and see each other more often so that the channels for discussion are open. Seven of the eleven sets of joint parents live within a fifteen-minute drive of each other, whereas half of the single parents had an ex who was out of town. This proximity could arguably increase the amount of conflict between parents because they have more opportunity to fight. But there is one feature of joint custody that definitely seems to invite less conflict. Recall that single mothers resented the fact that their ex-husbands had left them alone to raise the children without help of any kind. One fact that is clear is that the joint fathers are involved in their children's lives. Thus joint mothers may feel less anger toward their ex—anger that is often translated into a financial struggle. Whatever the reason for this difference in settling finances, it is *not* because joint parents are financially more comfortable than single parents, as table 3-1 showed. The joint mothers' incomes dropped as much as those of the low-education mothers—despite the fact that two-thirds of joint mothers are working professionals! Thus even if they have a more civil method for negotiating money troubles, it is still the case that joint mothers have little money to live on and thus rank money as their number 1 problem.

When asked about the types of problems that arise as a result of their incomes, joint mothers reported the same problems as single mothers. Their responses will be sketched next.

Work, Credit, and Moving

Joint mothers had more work-related problems than the fathers did. As with the single fathers, joint fathers had few changes in employment. Only one father changed jobs—and he is making much more money than before the divorce. Another father, in order to spend more time with his children, stopped working a part-time job he had held before the divorce. He reported that he felt "great" about this—both physically and emotionally.

Approximately half of the joint mothers had never held a full-time job before the divorce. Echoing the sentiments of some of the single-custody mothers, one woman explained:

I had stayed home with the children all my life. I had no skills and no self-confidence. I was a cleaning woman for a whole year. It was horrible—so depressing to do that kind of work. (Joint mother Z, split week.)

Three women had started college since the divorce. One had just finished school and was beginning a career. All reported that these changes had brought a mix of excitement, stress, and satisfaction. Only one—mother Z—reported that she would prefer to stay home and not work.

Again several women had problems with credit and other forms of discrimination:

I could easily get credit in his name now—but not in my own. He cosigned a car loan for me, and there was no problem. But I don't want to depend on that. That is completely emotionally wrong now! I want credit in my own name. (Joint mother X, split week.)

Eight of the nine joint mothers had moved out of the family house. Only one was bitterly unhappy about it. This was mother Z again—who had had to clean:

Moving from the suburbs to the projects was really hard. The projects are ugly, and there is no privacy; there is always someone at the window. There is no one here we can relate to. My teenage daughter especially hates it. She never invites anyone home. (Joint mother Z, student and secretary, children are five, twelve, and nine, split week.)

Six of the nine joint fathers moved. None expressed negative feelings about their new residences or about the moving process. In contrast to the mothers' problems, joint fathers described their money problems in terms of having fewer "extras":

Together we would be making $35,000 now. I lost her income. I would like to invest in real estate, but don't have the same capital. (Joint father B, college administrator, children are five and nine, split week.)

Another father remarked:

I have two-thirds of my married income. It doesn't make a difference in my lifestyle, but I don't save as much. (Joint father A, physicist, children are six and twelve, split week.)

Advantages

Approximately half the joint families reported that an important advantage of joint custody is that babysitters are not needed as often as they would be otherwise. These were parents who had been able to use their ex-spouses as sitters. They dated on the nights the children were in the other house. Parents reported that it was not only financially advantageous but also emotionally advantageous that they felt better about leaving the children with their other parent—who cared for them in a way a teenage sitter never could. This security allowed them not to feel guilty about going out to enjoy themselves.

The other advantages are identical with those cited by the single-custody parents. As in the case of single custody, joint mothers found many more advantages than joint fathers. Nearly half the joint mothers mentioned that they now had a job they enjoyed and that they would not have worked if not for the divorce. Over half mentioned that they liked feeling in control of resources. Here are two typical comments:

> It's fulfilling to have control over how money is spent. I have more self-respect now that I can buy the kids new shoes without asking his permission. Knowing that I can even buy myself something without asking his permission. I like being an adult. (Joint mother Z, student and secretary, children are five, nine, and twelve, split week.)

Joint mother A quipped:

> Yes I feel more in control of money. And if I had more money, I'd feel more in control!

Thus it would appear that in terms of economics, joint custody has some advantages over single custody. As mentioned before, parents say joint custody is cheaper because it seems to lead to fewer court battles than single custody. Perhaps this is due to the fact that joint parents realize that they will need to remain in close contact with their ex-spouses and that they simply could not emotionally afford to launch a court battle with this person. Instead, they settle their differences civilly. Third, we noted that no joint father was delinquent in child support at the time of the interview whereas delinquent support was the norm among single-custody mothers. If only because children unsupported by their fathers often become a burden on the taxpayer, joint custody would be an option worth exploring.

Conclusion: The Economics of Divorced Motherhood

One purpose of this study was to identify the problems and needs specific to single women and men in order to make recommendations for services. One unequivocal conclusion that these data provide is that women need access to information that will help them (1) to negotiate a fair settlement and (2) to manage money as a single parent. The fact that some women were unable to explain the settlement in the interview, that they had settled for insufficient child support because they did not know their husband's income, and that they failed to prod their less-than-helpful lawyers until they got the service they were paying for—all argue for the importance of courses that teach women their rights and of support groups through which women help each other in pushing for those rights. Such groups have already begun to spring up at YWCAs, women's studies centers, and churches.

A more complicated issue concerns the fact that one-quarter of the women in the sample had waived alimony. Their reason for having done so was something like, "I don't mind him supporting the children, but I don't want him giving gifts to me." At first this reasoning might appear to indicate that some consciousness raising had been achieved with regard to the consequences of economic dependence on men. Such a position contains a large blind spot, however, An insight is provided by John Kenneth Galbraith:

> The value of the services of housewives has been calculated at one fourth of the total Gross National Product. However, the labor of women to facilitate consumption is not valued in the national income or product. This is of some importance for its disguise: what is not counted is not often noticed. . .[3]

Pursuing Galbraith's thought—it is fascinating that the work of a governess or cleaning women *is* counted in the Gross National Product, but if such an employee marries her employer, the same work is no longer counted.[4] There are those today who believe in Virginia Woolf's 1938 proposition that a "wage" should be "paid by the State to those whose profession is marriage and motherhood."[5]

When I presented to the women who had waived alimony the idea that they had contributed their labor toward the marriage for many years, enabling their husbands to go out and work, they replied that they had "never thought of it that way." Changing women's economic situation will of course entail more than changing credit and other laws. Socialization runs so deep that many women do not fight even when the laws are fair. Two astute authors on this subject have written that:

> From childhood, a man is programmed for a life of financial responsibility. It is interwoven with his self image and success image. . . . In contrast, women perform the functions of consumption and household management. . . . They are taught that their roles are supportive and subject to the needs and desires of their families.[6]

The results of this chapter predict much of what is to come in the ensuing chapters. The centrality of economics was crystalized by Michael Harrington in *The Other America*: "Being poor is not one aspect of a person's life in this country, it *is* his life.''[7] We have already seen some of the consequences of the divorced mothers' financial straits. As the other family functions are discussed, it will become clear how economic problems invade every other aspect of women's lives.

Notes

1. *National NOW Times* 1981 *14* (7) ERA and the 59c Wage Gap.

2. For a comprehensive discussion of women's economic disadvantages, see D. Ahern and B. Bliss, *The Economics of Being a Woman* (New York: McGraw-Hill, 1976).

3. John Kenneth Galbraith, *Economics and the Public Purpose* (Boston: Houghton Mifflin, 1973).

4. Ahern and Bliss, *Economics of Being a Woman*, p. 3.

5. Virginia Woolf, *Three Guineas* (New York: Harcourt, Brace and World, 1963).

6. Ahern and Bliss, *Economics of Being a Woman*, p. 2.

7. M. Harrington, *The Other America* (Baltimore: Penguin Books, 1962), p. 17.

4 Authority

Married parents have the responsibility of defining the limits of their children's behavior and of enforcing rules that express those limits. There are many ways in which parents collaborate to exercise authority in a family. In some cases they share the task equally. In other cases there is a division of labor such that one parent is the lawgiver and the other is the enforcer. In still other families, one parent does most of the disciplining, utilizing the partner only as a consultant or "backup." Any of these configurations can be used successfully or unsuccessfully in the two-parent home. Regardless of how parental authority is organized during a marriage, it must be reorganized after divorce. Divorce can make disciplining children easier, more difficult, or both—but there is no way that it can *not* make a difference. To reiterate the book's premise: The dissolution of the marital dyad influences how the family performs each of its functions.

The ways in which custodial mothers, fathers, and joint parents in this study reorganized their parental authority was of particular interest. Folk wisdom on the nuclear family has it that children need a resident father to keep them in line. Recall that divorced mothers were confronted with this maxim while searching for apartments. Landlords told them, "Without a man around, kids run wild." A few fathers faced discrimination in housing based on their marital status, but none were told that "kids run wild" without a mother in the home.

The landlords are not alone in their opinions. As pointed out in chapter 1, there is an extensive literature attempting to link father absence to all types of problems—especially to school failure and delinquency. These studies were criticized for their generally poor socioeconomic controls.

Recently, however, Mavis Hetherington and her colleagues did a rigorous observational study in which they found that middle-class preschool children obeyed their fathers' commands more often than their mothers' commands after divorce. Children were observed as they interacted with each parent alone in a waiting room. At the two-year follow-up, the children were still more compliant with their fathers than with their mothers.

Is there a truth buried in the rumor that children living without a father run wild? If so, how can the difference between mothers' and fathers' success in disciplining be explained? These questions are addressed in this chapter.

Let us begin with the question of locus of responsibility. The first question is: Within this sample, how did the husband-wife team organize their parental authority before the divorce, and how is it done now?

Locus of Responsibility:
Single-Custody Parents

More than two-thirds of the single-custody mothers had shouldered the major responsibility for disciplining the children prior to the divorce and had relied on their husbands for back-up (table 4-1). A few mothers reported that their husbands had been in charge of disciplining, and an even smaller number reported that both parents had shared this task. Each of the mothers stated that since the divorce, they have had full responsibility for disciplining the children. The mothers felt that the burden was greater now than before because they had lost their consulting partner. Only two mothers felt comfortable even discussing a discipline issue occasionally with their ex-husbands.

The single fathers' situation is comparable. Half said they had been the primary disciplinarian prior to the divorce, and all felt that this was their job alone now that they were single parents. This is quite a contrast to the joint-custody parents who reported that they were actually sharing authority with their ex-spouse *more* since the divorce than before it. (Again, the joint families will be discussed separately at the end of the chapter).

Table 4-1
Who Disciplines?

Custodian	Time	*Myself (Percent)*	*My Ex (Percent)*	*Both of Us (Percent)*
Mothers[a]	Predivorce	69	19	12
	Postdivorce	100	—	—
Fathers[b]	Predivorce	50	12	38
	Postdivorce	100	—	—
Joint mothers[c]	Predivorce	66	11	22
	Postdivorce	11	11	77
Joint fathers[d]	Predivorce	44	44	11
	Postdivorce	11	22	66

[a] Pre-post difference is significant. $X^2(2) = 7.27$; $p < .05$.
[b] Pre-post difference is significant. $X^2(2) = 16$; $p < .001$.
[c] Pre-post difference is significant. $X^2(2) = 17.66$; $p < .001$.
[d] Pre-post difference is significant. $X^2(2) = 28.25$; $p < .001$.

What types of change would we expect in parents' methods of disciplining children when responsibility shifts from two adults to one? One could argue that discipline would need to become more rigorous in order to compensate for the absent parent. One could argue, on the other hand, that discipline would need to be relaxed since children would in most cases need to be more responsibile for themselves. Here is how single mothers and fathers answered the question, "How did your style of discipline change after the divorce?"

Changes in Style

The Mothers

Three-quarters of the mothers reported that they had become stricter after the divorce. A few said they had become more lenient. Even fewer said their style had not changed at all. There was a great variety of reasons for mothers' changes in style. The most common reasons for changing style had to do with having less time and energy as a result of working two jobs or longer hours since the divorce. Thus their economic situations became important determinants of how they exercised authority. Some mothers translated it into a necessity to do more, and some to do less or different disciplining:

> I am much stricter now—much less patient. I demand more from the children because I am working and going to school and need their help with the house. I used to be enormously permissive with them, but I no longer have the energy or time to discuss the same issue fifty-five times. (Paralegal, children are ten, fourteen, and sixteen.)

Said another mother:

> I've become stricter because when I get home from the hospital, I'm tired and can't put up with a lot of stuff. So I make more rules and stick to them. (L.P.N., children are four and eight.)

The mother who had moved back in with her parents emphasized the need to be firm with her son in a houshold where everyone else wanted to spoil him:

> My parents are indulging grandparents, and I have to be really strict in order to balance them. I spell out rules for him very clearly—in their presence if possible—so that they also know I mean business. (Secretary, son is four.)

One mother spoke of having become much stricter with her son (then seven) immediately after the divorce out of her own need to feel that she was in control of things. This woman felt she was completely alone in a very demanding world. To ward off the feeling that things were falling apart, she became very organized in her own life—and also began organizing the details of her children's lives. Her son reacted to this angrily, and she loosened the reins:

> In the beginning I was much stricter. I held on to them like they were going to disappear. I was so afraid that they would get hurt, and it was my responsibility—now it was all mine. I wouldn't let them do things they had been allowed to do before. My son got really hyper as a result. He wasn't allowed to go down the street. I was overprotective—frightened probably. I see now he needed more rope; he needed to be out with his friends (L.P.N., children are four and eight.)

The children in these families were aware of the change in their mothers' disciplining. The son of the mother just quoted said, for example:

> First, when my mom and dad were married, I was allowed to do more stuff. Like I could stay overnight at my friend's, and cross Main Street at a light. And I was only six then, and then when I was seven my mother wouldn't let me. I think she wanted to be meaner to make up for my Dad being gone because he was a little meaner than her. (Boy, eight.)

There were other children as well who related their mother's increased strictness to their father's absence:

> My mother got much stricter since the divorce. She used to let dad do all the spanking. She was always nice, and he was the one we were scared of. She started to be harder after the divorce. She had to—because he wasn't around anymore. (Girl, ten.)

One child, now in his father's custody, cited his mother's lax discipline as an important reason leading to the switch from her custody to his:

> We lived with my mother right after the divorce. It started out OK, but she was depressed a lot. She wasn't effective in disciplining us as Dad is, so we didn't obey her. We talked back and did what we wanted. She got fed up with it and decided we should live with our father. (Boy, twelve.)

Not all children accepted the necessity of stricter discipline philosophically:

> I miss my Dad being here because he used to do stuff our Mom wouldn't let us do. Like if she said you can't have that toy—it's too dangerous—we could say, "Aw Dad, can't we have it?" and he would say yes. (Boy, nine.)

A few mothers actually became more lenient after the divorce. These mothers tended to have older children, who would have begun to require more autonomy regardless of the marital dissolution. Said one mother of teenagers:

> As I have gotten older, I have become more lenient. My kids know if they are responsible, I won't come down hard on them. I don't give them strict home times. (High school teacher, children are eleven, fourteen, fifteen, and seventeen.)

Another mother attributed her more laissez-faire discipline to the fact that the household was now a more relaxed place without her ex-husband:

> They are older and don't need it as much. It's also a more relaxed household now. He was a tense person. He would give them the belt, and I was not to interfere. (Nonworking librarian, children are eleven, thirteen, and fourteen.)

One mother had initially become more indulgent with her children in order to compete favorably with their father who spent his visits wining and dining them. When this led to serious acting out in her fourteen-year-old son, she began setting firm limits:

> My oldest boy was really out of hand. I was afraid of disciplining them for fear they'd hate me more because I didn't buy them things and take them fancy places like him. I just got up my courage and started telling my son: You will be back in this house at ten P.M. on the dot. I was absolutely shocked, but he did it! (Avon representative, children are ten, fifteen, and sixteen.)

Several mothers felt that the words *stricter* and *more lenient* did not adequately describe the change in their disciplining style. Some felt their styles had changed in complex and subtle ways.

> It's different. It used to be spankings. Now it is geared to fit our new lifestyle. With me working and going to school, I have to be more trusting than before because they have to depend on themselves more. When I do something, I try to explain it. I treat them like people, not children. It changed when I began working full time and going to school. (Student and secretary, children are seven, ten, and eleven.)

Several mothers related changes in their parenting to changes they had experienced in themselves after the divorce:

> I'm more reasonable with them now. I was harder on the kids when he was around because I was uptight all the time. I would say, "Go to your room and don't bother me." I learned you got to listen to your kid. This has

come from feeling better as a person. From being a better person, really. (Unemployed mother, daughters are thirteen and fourteen.)

The daughter of this mother commented:

My mother is much easier on us now. She used to yell and scream all the time. She is much happier since the divorce so she is nicer to us and lets us do more things like get our ears pierced. Also we're older now. (Girl, thirteen.)

Another teen-aged girl crystallized aptly the situation that existed in several of these homes after the divorce:

It's a completely different situation now. You can't compare them. When my parents were together, one of them would say, "Do this," and we would gripe and balk about it. We weren't that close a family. But now we're very close, and we don't balk about things—even the little kids don't. It's not that mom is stricter—to answer your question. But with her working, everyone has to pull together and do their best. (Girl, sixteen.)

The Fathers

In contrast to the majority of mothers who felt they had become stricter after the divorce, the majority of single fathers reported that they had become more lenient disciplinarians after the divorce. Their reasons were intriguingly uniform. They revolved around wanting to be kind to their children in order to compensate for the emotional loss brought by the separation:

There is a tendency to feel guilty about the fact that their mother is not here. I give them more leniency. I rarely hit them. I try to reason with them. I feel guilty. It's my fault they don't have a mother. I am extremely lenient. Luckily my kids are good kids. Disciplining them is never a big deal. (Machinist, children are eleven, twelve, and fourteen.)

A father with younger children said:

If anything, I'm easier. I'm trying to make up for their loss. It is a loss to them; it would have to be. I don't want to come home from work and jump all over them right away for the stuff they pulled all day and are going to pull the next day, 'cause it wouldn't take long and they would hate to see me come through the door. (Mechanic, daughters are four, eight, twelve, and thirteen.)

One father said he had become more lenient in contrast to his overly punitive style developed during an unhappy marriage:

I used to punch them—I mean worse than a spanking. I was much too harsh on them. Now I reason with them. I almost feel now like I took out on them the anger I felt for my wife. Those punches were really meant for her. (Lawyer, sons are twelve and fourteen.)

Approximately one-fourth of the fathers articulated this relaxed style of authority in terms of a shift in their relationship with the child—almost from a filial to a companionate relationship:

I used to do the old-fashioned thrashing—but no more. I'm more lenient. I feel very bad because of the divorce. I bleed for them. He's gone through enough as it is. I feel sometimes that there is nobody in the world but me and Marty—so how can I discipline Marty! I may punish him, but it eats away at me, and I remove the punishment. We're more like buddies now. We talk all the time. I can confide in him. It's not like before when I was a husband and had a wife to confide in, and he was a kid. (Sales manager, son is thirteen).

It was a little surprising to find that even the father of a seven-year-old conceived of his relationship with his son as a "partnership":

I'm easier than I would be with two parents in this house. It's he and I; he's my partner in our twosome—so it's important that he love me. I am more reluctant to discipline him. I'm indulgent—but at least I'm aware of it. (Professor, son is seven.)

Nor did this kind of partnership develop only between fathers and sons. Here are the comments of the father of a seven-year-old girl:

I'm easier now—not as rigid. I feel closer to her now. We're a family even though it's just the two of us. I feel bad when I have to discipline her. (Business executive, daughter is seven.)

It is possible for parents to befriend their children too much. I have seen parents in therapy who view it as an act of disloyalty when their child chooses the company of peers over their own. In some cases, children who have been a parent's confidant feel extremely protective of that parent and have a hard time separating from him or her. Such excesses did not seem apparent in the families in this study. The children referred to in the last three quotes, for example, appeared to be well adjusted. They were all doing well in school and had active social lives with peers. Their fathers also had well-developed support groups, and by no means relied on their children alone for friendship. In these cases, the father-child companionship seemed to be working to the benefit of all. The thirteen-year-old son of the sales manager said:

My dad and I are like buddies. We look out for each other. I try to stay out of trouble, and not to make waves. He does extra stuff for me, like make

pizza or something. And we talk a whole lot now. Like in the evenings
when he comes home from work, we'll talk and take a walk.

Some fathers, like the mothers, felt their change in style of discipline was
not unidirectional. This is illustrated in the following quote, through which
we again hear the theme of children as companions:

> In some ways I'm stricter and in some ways more lenient. I try to give them
> as much voice as possible in the way the family moves. They are the reason
> this family exists. If we were married, it would be the couple making the
> decisions and the kids following. But now I say: "This is what I want to do;
> what do you want to do?" Things like what to cook and which sitters to
> have and how to spend Sunday. (Toolmaker, children are eight and nine.)

According to conventional sex roles, women are kinder, more compas-
sionate people, and men are firmer and more task oriented. These results
suggest that mothers after divorce move in the direction of the conventional
male role and that fathers adopt a more "womanly" style. This tendency
suggests that parents of both sexes come to acquire a broader repertoire of
responses after divorce—by internalizing the behavior of the absent parent.
Such a process might serve as one definition of successful coping.

Are Two Authorities Better than One?

The Mothers

Parents were asked to reflect on their role as disciplinarians at the present
and during the marriage, and then they were asked the question, "Do you
feel that two parents could discipline your children more effectively than
you alone?"

Fully three-quarters of the mothers felt that being a single disciplinarian
was stressful and that there were clear benefits to having two resident adults
to perform the task. The modal reason for this had to do with the personal
stamina it takes to perform this function continuously:

> In Jasmine's case, yes, I have felt disciplining to be overwhelming—not
> with the others. Since she was twelve she has considered herself my equal.
> She is very bright, lazy, and headstrong and very hard for me to handle. It's
> a question of numbers, and two adults would have an easier time of it.
> (Paralegal, children are ten, fourteen, and sixteen.)

One mother was particularly candid about her feelings of being overwhelmed by raising two teenagers alone:

I have told them twice I would like to get in the car and never come back. Since my daughter started high school, her mouth has not shut. She talks constantly and that can get to you terribly. But I'm with them twenty-four hours a day. I need a vacation! (Unemployed mother, daughters are thirteen and fourteen.)

One mother pointed out that feeling overwhelmed affected the quality of her disciplining:

You get tired of being on your toes all the time. One day I'll yell at them for jumping on the beds, and the next day I'll let it slide because I'm too tired to yell. This means I'm less consistent, and consistency is important. (Student and secretary, children are seven, ten, and eleven.)

Other mothers complained about feeling like the "meanie," which, although it might not affect their competence as parents, was nevertheless demoralizing:

I'm the bad parent because I do the disciplining. The kids resent my should-nots. He buys them CBs and bikes, and I tell them when to come in and to do their chores. (Avon representative, children are ten, fifteen, and sixteen.)

Another concern was about needing another adult's opinion about an important decision for a child:

My daughter goes to modeling school and wanted to drive there with her sixteen-year-old friend who just got her license. I wanted Kay to go very much but was worried about them driving that distance. I talked to my ex about it. He said he felt the same concern but would probably let her go. It's hard to make a decision alone that concerns danger or the welfare of your child. On something like that I will still consult him. He doesn't mind at all. (Graduate student and secretary, children are sixteen and eighteen.)

Still another consideration was that it might be easier on the child to have another parent as a buffer:

I think the intensity of having one parent and not having two perspectives makes it harder for the child. I know from living with my lover a few years back that there were things that bugged me that didn't bug him, and so it's nice for a kid's sake to have another person around. (Assistant professor, daughter is seven.)

In view of the cultural cliché that children need their father's discipline, I asked mothers specifically if they felt a man could discipline their children more effectively. Three mothers offered some type of affirmative response to this question:

A man's voice is deeper and louder. They're immune to my voice. (Unemployed mother, children are six and nine.)

Said another:

My son seems to respect a man more. He listens to his father more than me. And when my boyfriend gives an order, he jumps whereas I have to say it five times. (L.P.N., children are four and eight.)

The remaining mothers felt that although two parents might be better than one, it was two adults who were needed, and not necessarily a male:

It would be nice to have another perspective, but that has nothing to do with needing a male perspective. Certainly my children are better behaved now than when they had the benefit of *his* male perspective. (Therapy aid, children are ten and fifteen.)

Another mother summarized several of the discipline issues cogently:

I used to think that before he left, but not now. He had me convinced a man could do everything better. I was afraid I wouldn't carry the respect he had. But I realized I was going to have to fill his shoes; nobody else was going to do it. I found that as I got more confidence in myself and more self-respect that other people—including my children—began to see me as a strong person. (Unemployed librarian, children are eleven, thirteen, and fourteen.)

The Fathers

Nearly all the single fathers believed that two parents could discipline children more effectively than one. Note that neither the fathers nor the mothers felt that the noncustodial parent had any responsibility for disciplining the children. As one father said, whose thirteen-year-old son sees his mother weekly, "She's not disciplining him when she's taking him bowling." There is, of course, a modicum of responsibility incumbent on visiting parents when they take their children on weekends. Misbehavior in a bowling alley or art museum must in some way be dealt with. The father just quoted, however, clearly was referring to a larger, more complex set of parental decisions through which a parent determines the degree of autonomy a given child can master. It is the custodial parent, and not the visitor, after all, who must agonize over whether a teen can get a driver's license or a nine-year-old can play football or a six-year-old can cross the street alone.

The concern that mothers had about seeming like the ogre was virtually absent from the fathers' accounts. Furthermore, no father described disciplining the children as "overwhelming" as the mothers often did. The fathers' reasons for preferring two disciplining parents had to do with the availability of another adult to share the load:

> If two parents are getting on well, they can do a better job. One can relieve the other while the other recharges their emotional battery. (Machinist, children are eleven, twleve, and fourteen.)

Other fathers spoke of the value of a second parent in tempering the style of the other when it became too strong or too lax:

> We get up at seven and have to be out of here at eight. Ralph walks into walls in the morning, and one morning I yelled at him and felt bad all day. The disadvantage of being the only one is having to dole it out and then make up for it. There wasn't anyone else there to temper the anger and make him feel better. (High school principal, children are twelve and fourteen.)

None of the fathers felt that a woman could discipline the children more effectively than a man could.

Children's Role in Changing the Authority Structure

The way in which the absent parent's authority is compensated is, of course, influenced by how the children are acting. Massive acting out in children after divorce may lead the custodial parent to become much stricter or to invest some parental authority in an older child.

As was discussed in chapter 1, the children in this sample did little serious acting out. Only two children out of ninety-three had become involved in what could be considered antisocial behavior (that is, truancy, drug use, and so on). The "behavior problems" of the other children were on the order of talking back and refusing to do chores. Parents were asked to what extent their children had become more difficult to discipline after divorce.

The Mothers

Over half of the mothers belived that one or more of their children had begun testing their authority after the divorce. Only a few mothers, however, felt that this testing was still occurring two to three years after the divorce. Here are some of their comments:

> For a while he just wasn't doing his chores and was snapping back at me. I had to become firmer so that didn't get out of hand. I think he wanted to know that I was really going to be there to guide him—that he still had a parent. That phase lasted a few months. (Nurse, son is nine.)

Another mother said:

> Not my daughter, but my seven-year-old son pushed me a lot. He was angry at me because he didn't know why his father had left, and he blamed a lot on me that I made his Dad go. It's still a problem now, but it's much better. He was getting into fights at school and was always in trouble in the neighborhood. (L.P.N., children are four and eight.)

One mother who had a daughter now in her twenties (who was not in the study) referred to a serious problem that that daughter had which she, the mother, attributed to ineffective handling of authority issues:

> I have an older daughter, now married, who was seventeen when we were splitting up, and she started drinking and would come home drunk. I became very protective, and she rebelled against me. I was in a bad emotional state myself because of the break-up. I was in no position to give her what she needed. There was a great rift created between us, and we didn't speak for years. She has had other problems since then—a bad marriage of her own. I feel we could have saved her all that if it weren't for the divorce and the way I handled it. (Store manager, son is fifteen, at home).

The other half of the single mothers felt that their children had demonstrated no appreciable change in their response to authority since the divorce, and one reported that her son was much better behaved since the divorce because she said, "He was out of all that storm and stress of the marriage and became a happy kid."

Several of the children were old enough and perceptive enough to explain their change in behavior after the divorce. Said one girl who had waged war with her mother for an entire year:

> My mother and I had terrible fights. I went to school crying every day in eighth grade. I was going through teen-age independence too fast. She bothered me a lot and I bothered her too. I felt the divorce was her fault—that she had nagged my dad out of pure selfishness. I thought he was Mr. Perfect. I wanted my mother to feel like an "ick." I feel bad about that now. (Girl, sixteen.)

This family decided that Jasmine should go to live with her father at that time. She was even unhappier there—ironically, because he gave her too much independence:

> I went to live with my dad, knowing that he wouldn't be on top of me all the time. She used to want to know every move I made. Anyhow, the problem with my dad was he let me do anything I wanted at any hour as long as I told him where I was. But he never left notes about where he was. I didn't feel a sense of security at my dad's house.

Jasmine was at that point in a real dilemma. She wanted to return to her mother's house but did not want to appear defeated. She told me that the adults handled the situation well:

> My dad knew I wanted to go back but that I didn't want to admit it. So he came out and asked me if I was ready to switch again—saying that my mother had told him it was all right. That took the load off me. This is four years ago now. My mother and I still fight—don't get me wrong. But we respect each other and treat each other as human beings.

Jasmine was one of many sensitive and articulate children in the study. Ernie, although only nine, also had insight into his fighting:

> I was real mad when he left. Every time a kid called me names, I would give him a bloody nose. I still get real mad. My dad goes away on business all the time and Ma works and goes to school. I don't get to do many fun things now.

This child's mother was terrified when her husband left. She was afraid that without any job skills she would not be able to support her two young children, and went through several months of depression. She talked of calling a phone number for parents who are afraid they might abuse their children and was relieved to know that her feelings were not unique to her. In the two years since her husband left, she has put her life in order, and her son's fighting at school is now much more infrequent.

The Fathers

Only one-quarter of the fathers felt that their children had initiated more discipline-worthy behavior after the divorce. (Fifty-six percent of the mothers had seen a change for the worse. The difference is statistically significant). This difference between maternal and paternal children is also reflected in answers to two other questions. The first was, "Do the children play off you and your ex?"

The Mothers

Approximately one-third of the mothers reported this playing off as a problem. In each of those cases the children were seeing their fathers on a regular basis. (In cases in which children never see their fathers, this manipulation would obviously not be possible.)

> My son will say, "I can do that at father's," and I say, "Father has his rules and I have mine." This has been hard to get across to him. Bedtime is one thing, and the amount of TV, and how far outside the house he can go. His father lives in the suburbs, and Ernie has the run of the place. This is the city, and I can't let him go as far. Both of us reinforce the fact that there are two separate rules. When I drop them off, we will both mention that. (L.P.N., children are four and nine.)

One mother spoke of helping the child discriminate between the two houses. Emphasizing the fact that the child was *confused* enabled this mother to see her task as one of clarifying boundaries and not of punishing a stubborn child. Here are her words:

> She started early saying, "I don't have to do that at Dad's," and so I started immediately helping her to differentiate the two households. Instead of saying, "But you're not getting away with that crap here," I just said, "That's something you can look forward to at Dad's," and this has worked well. (Assistant professor, daughter is seven.)

A corollary to this question is, "Are they more difficult to handle when they return from a visit?" One-quarter of the mothers reported having some problems with this:

> Because of the two sets of rules—with TV, roaming the neighborhood and bedtime—he is tense when he first returns from his dad's. I guess I just let it wear off. (L.P.N. children are four and nine.)

Another mother said:

> My big problem is that he doesn't enforce bedtime, and she comes back irritable and hard to be with. It's not worth bringing it up to him; I would only get defensive denial. (Assistant professor, daughter is seven.)

One mother made the mistake of grilling her children about their father after a visit:

> Right after the divorce I was so hurt that he had left me, and I was curious about his new life and if he was really happy. So when the kids came home, I would quiz them. I wanted to find out if they liked her better. They didn't

like answering these questions, so they would come home already closed up to me, and I would quiz them anyway, and there would be a big fight. (Avon representative, children are ten, fifteen, and sixteen.)

Fathers

In terms of children playing off parents and being harder to handle after visits, fathers again had an easier time of it than mothers. Only 19 percent of the fathers complained about children playing off their parents:

The daughter who is not in my custody does this. She would tell her mother that I let her to do things she couldn't do there. So my ex called me and said, "Talk to her!" She would threaten to move in with me if her mother didn't let her do things. I had a talk alone with her and said, "You respect your mother," and it has been better since. (Security guard, children are thirteen and fourteen.)

Only one father had noticed a problem with transitions between households, and he has developed a good strategy for coping with it:

When they would return from their Saturday morning visit to her, they would seem a little wound up. Then I would leave for work forty-five minutes later and leave them with a sitter all day. Now I make them stay in the house with me a little while so I can see them and they can wind down. They don't like visiting her, and it makes them tense. (Toolmaker, children are eight and nine.)

Despite the variety of problems of being the solo disciplinarian, there are also some advantages, to be discussed next.

**Advantages to Disciplining as
a Single Parent**

Approximately one-half of the mothers and one-half of the fathers felt that disciplining the children had been an issue for struggle during the marriage and that everyone was better off now that that conflict was absent.

We fought about disciplining them. I'm open, and he's tight and controlled. I would allow them to say "I'm mad at you," and he'd punish them for it. I have some tough problems with the kids, but it was worse when he was here. (Unemployed mother, children are six and nine.)

Said another mother:

I would tell Ted to take a bath, and my ex-husband would pop up and say—no, he doesn't have to take a bath. Of course the bath had nothing to do with it—it was just an excuse for my ex to start a fight. But in the meantime, whatever Ted did was taking sides with one of us. (Avon representative, children are ten, fifteen, and sixteen.)

One father cited the mother's behavior as a stimulus to the child's misbehavior:

She drank from noon until bedtime. I know I'm more irritable after a few beers. Her discipline was more like revenge. At that time Joey was fighting a lot; he was in trouble in school for punching, hitting, and throwing rocks. I feel he mimicked her aggression, because he has stopped that. I have more patience with him than she did. (Machinist, children are eleven, twelve, and fourteen.)

It is interesting that common arguments against joint custody are that children cannot adapt to two sets of rules, that they will play off their parents, and that there will be transition problems as they move from one house to the other. As we shall see, however, the authority problems of the joint parents are not very different from those of the single-custody parents just described.

Joint-Custody Families

Who Disciplines?

Joint-custody parents were asked, "Who was responsible for disciplining children before the divorce, and who is responsible now?" Their answers form quite a contrast to the single parents' where the trend went from having some shared responsibility to sharing much less after divorce. In contrast, more joint mothers and fathers reported sharing authority after the divorce than before (refer again to table 4-1). This is evidence that joint parenthood involved not merely fun time spent with one parent, but total parenting by both adults. The fact that both mothers and their ex-husbands reported that this was the case makes it less likely that these responses are simply the wishful thinking of parents who are actually peripheral.

There is one case in which the parents' accounts were contradictory. Here is what the mother said about discipline:

I did all the disciplining in the marriage because he was always working, and he went out a lot at night. It was all left in my lap. Now we each do it—depending on which house they're at. (Family Z, children are five, nine, and twleve.)

Here is the account of her ex-husband:

> Nothing has changed. I'm still mostly responsible for disciplining the children. She never did it—and it used to aggravate the hell out of me. It was easier for her not to do anything. I still am the only one who disciplines them. She would let them get away with anything. I've told them, "You respect her while you're over there or I'll take care of you, just like it was here."

This is one of the problematic joint-custody families in which the mother had felt forced into the joint arrangement and wanted to get out of it. The disparity in their accounts reflects the fact that they have not worked out their differences as well as the other joint families who also had sustained high conflict in their marriages.

Discipline Style

Parents were asked if their style of discipline had changed since the divorce and why. Recall that single-custody mothers tended to become stricter, and fathers became more lenient. The modal response of both joint mothers and fathers, however, was "no change." In other words, they had not changed their style of discipline after the divorce. This makes sense if we adhere to the notion that the single parents changed their styles in order to bring to their disposal the skills of the absent parent. In the joint-custody families, neither parent is absent. In addition, whereas the majority of single mothers and fathers felt that two resident parents could discipline more effectively, only a minority of joint parents felt that parents in an intact home could do a better job of disciplining than they. Again, this difference is most probably due to the fact that joint custody more closely approximates the intact family than does single-parent custody.

Two Sets of Rules

In only one case did joint-custody parents actually consult each other regularly in order to make decisions about discipline. In that family, parents discussed the best bedtime for their toddler so that she had a consistent life schedule. Also, when their teenage son had a school problem, they conferred about what to do. This was very comfortable for them as they described themselves as "still close friends." The majority of joint parents did *not* call each other to discuss these issues. Instead, the norm was, "I have my rules; he has his."

All the joint-custody parents felt that there were some rules that were different in the two houses. The majority of these parents reported that their children had at some points attempted to abuse this difference by playing off the parents. Fewer joint parents than single-custody fathers, however, reported this problem. As was the case with the single-custody families, the joint parents stated that this type of manipulation had decreased over time. Here are some descriptions of the problems of joint discipline and how parents coped with them:

> There are two sets of rules regarding bedtimes and cleaning of rooms. Also, Butch got a slingshot for his birthday which he knew his mother would never let him have. I said, "If I hear one complaint that you've used it there, out it goes." And, of course, I told his mother, "You're going to hate it, but I bought Butch a slingshot. She said, "You're right I hate it. Make sure he uses it there." A few times they have tried the playing off stuff, and I have said, "Unh unh. That's shopping for a decision. Illegal." (Joint father A, sons are six and twelve, split week.)

The view of joint mother A was consistent with that of her ex-husband:

> He lets them do stuff with knives—things I feel are too dangerous—and they have no bedtime there. Once in awhile a kid will say, "Dad lets me," and I say, "Not in this house." It's not a big problem, but it's there.

Only rarely, it seems, would one parent intercede with the other for permission to do something in the other house. Here is an example:

> They have to go to bed really early there, and sometimes they complain they can't watch a worthwhile TV show. I will occasionally call in advance to ask him if they could stay up a bit later to watch it. Sometimes it works and sometimes it doesn't. I hesitate to do it lest it seem to him or his wife that I am trying to run their show. (Joint mother C, real-estate agent, children are nine and ten, split day.)

One mother saw the two-rules issue as insignificant:

> There are two sets of rules, but they've always had that because Grandma's rules were different at her house. What was really tough was when my mother and I were in the same house. Whose rules applied then? Now when they say, "Dad lets us," I just say "That's Dad." (Joint mother X, social worker, children are six, seven, nine, ten, and twelve, split week.)

Thus the joint parents have slightly different ways of dealing with the two-rule situation. They have in common, however, a respect for the authority of the other parent, and the ability confidently to explain their policy to their children.

There were occasional problems that resulted when a parent tried to make a rule for the other house:

> There was a time when my ex was upset about Mike's behavior, and he wanted to come down hard on him, and he made some rules, like be in at eleven P.M., and so on. He wasn't there to enforce them, however. I didn't feel that way about the situation, so I wasn't going to enforce his rules. What happend was, Mike conformed voluntarily. He respects his father very much. I didn't enforce the rule, but Mike just started coming in earlier. (Joint mother G, occupational therapist, children are eleven and fifteen, "unstructured.")

Although the G parents had a lot of contact with each other, they did not agree on how to handle Mike's behavior. In this case, things worked out fine, but one can see the potential danger. What if the mother had stressed to her son that father's rule was irrelevant to her? Mike could have found himself in the middle of a parental power struggle. There were two families in which such a struggle was operative. These were problematic joint families X and Z.

> The two sets of rules has led to confusion. I get a lot of flack about the different bedtimes. Also, my four-year-old just takes off here like she can over there. I would never discuss it with him. He would start a fight over it, and I want to stay my distance with him. (Joint mother Z, student and waitress, children are four, nine, and twelve.)

Her ex-husband felt that there were no problems with the two-rule set-up, although he did cite an example that seems consistent with mother's complaint:

> We had planned this camping trip, and the oldest one says she doesn't want to go. So I say, "OK, call your mother and see if she'll keep you." She does, and of course her mother says she doesn't have to go. At that point I say, "Wait a minute. This can't go on like this, or first thing you know, everything one of us asks them to do, they'll be on the phone to the other one." So I got everybody together, and we voted on how to spend the weekend. Cathy was outvoted, so we went camping. And, of course, she enjoyed it more than anyone. (Joint father Z, insurance salesman, children are four, nine, and twelve.)

Transition Problems

Over one-third of the joint parents had noticed a transition problem with their children. The solutions that they devised to make those transitions smoothe are typified by this idea:

I noticed they were a little sulky when they came here directly from their mother's, so I decided to do something with them right away to get them in the spirit of being here. We go for a walk or read the funnies or do something. (Joint father B, college administrator, children are five and nine, split week.)

Children's Feelings about Two Rules

All the joint children were aware that each parent had different rules for them to follow. Only one child out of twenty-five complained that this was currently creating a problem for her. This is the nine-year-old quoted in chapter 2 who felt caught between her parent's beliefs about health. Her father earnestly believed that he was doing the best thing for his child in removing sugar from her diet. Her mother, however, viewed his attitude as fanatical and faddish and was certainly not about to change her own habits to suit an ex-spouse. The result was that the daughter was often chided by her father about eating cookies at her mother's. Conversely, the child was occasionally treated to a sarcastic comment from her mother about father's eccentrism. This is complicated by the fact that father's health regimine was something initiated by the woman he had just married. It is not unreasonable to conclude that the two philosophies about health included a power struggle between the father's wife and ex-wife, with father somehow orchestrating the struggle. If this problem were emblematic of the way the family lived, it would mean disaster for the children. It seemed, however, to be the only snag in an otherwise smoothe arrangement. The child in question was in favor of joint custody and reported no other problems with it. The situation is useful in illustrating the necessity of confining rules to a given household.

None of the other joint children disliked having to follow two sets of rules. Influenced by warnings that "following two masters" would be psychologically impossible for children, I was careful to ask each of them, "Is it ever confusing or upsetting to have to follow one set of rules at Mom's and another at Dad's?" Most of the children answered very matter-of-factly that it was "not a big deal." One adolescent, in fact, appeared slightly insulted by the question:

Look. When you're in school all day, don't you have to behave different than when you're at home? Even in first grade? And I'm going on thirteen.

Is Disciplining the Children ever Overwhelming?

Only one joint father complained of feeling that disciplining the children was overwhelming. This was a father with two children who are based with

him ten months and spend the summer with their mother. His comments
sound like the single parents':

> I'll get absorbed in my work which I like to bring home, and if something
> goes wrong here with the kids and I have to straighten it out, I feel over-
> whelmed. Every parent needs a break. I don't have a mechanism for deal-
> ing with it yet. I can't go out and get drunk because they're here. (C.P.A.,
> sons are five and nine, split year.)

Advantages

As was the case with the single-custody parents, half of the joint parents
reported that an advantage of disciplining as a divorced parent was that the
disciplining was going on in an atmosphere of tranquility, as opposed to
violence. One-third of the parents, however, also mentioned that living in
two houses with their own laws and cultures would result in greater flexibility
in their children. For example:

> They've gotten a balance living with both of us. I'm more unstructured,
> and he's more structured. He has more rules. So if they have lived with only
> one of us, they wouldn't have been exposed to both. They are very flexibile
> kids. (Joint mother G, occupational therapist, children are eleven and fif-
> teen, "unstructured.")

The mother whose ex-husband advocated a health-food diet was ap-
preciative of his strengths:

> I'm not a good disciplinarian myself. I am not consistent. He is a very
> organized person and is fair and systematic with them. But there are other
> things they get from me that they don't get from him. I'm more likely to do
> cultural things with them; he hates concerts and museums. So they need
> both of us. I think complete exposure to either one of us would be bad for
> them. And this way, they get both of us. (Joint mother C, real-estate agent,
> children are nine and ten, split day.)

In summary, joint parenting does not necessitate regular consultation
between parents about disciplining children. Parents collaborated on the
disciplining of their children by respecting the right of the ex-spouse to
define acceptable behavior in his or her house. The fact that joint parents
were no more likely than single-custody parents to have collaborated on
discipline before the divorce is further evidence that joint parents were not
self-selected for an unusual ability to compromise.

Conclusions

This chapter began with a discussion of the stereotypes invoked by landlords who refuse to rent to single mothers. There is no evidence whatsoever in this study that without a resident father, children "run wild." Very few children in the entire sample had serious behavior problems, and those who did were distributed equally across custody types. The "testing of authority" in this chapter refers to children neglecting their chores, talking back, fussing about bedtime, and so on. In most cases, this behavior had diminished by the time of the interview.

Although children in maternal custody could hardly be called "wild," the mothers did report more problems than the fathers in the area of exercising authority. Single mothers were the only group in the study to describe this task as "overwhelming." Why should this be the case?

The results of this chapter are best interpreted in the light of the chapter on economics. Single mothers simply *are* the most overwhelmed group of divorced parents. Unlike single fathers, they have had to enter the job market for the first time and to support their family on a beginner's salary. Unlike the joint mothers, they cannot count on the child support from their ex-spouse or for a break from parenting. Adults who do not feel to be in control of their own lives are not in a good position appropriately to control the behavior of children. Kay Tooley (1975) has in fact suggested that the acting out of some children of divorce is a counterphobic response to the apprehension they sense in their mothers.

As mothers in this study made progress in coping with their financial problems, the testing and manipulation by the children diminished.

Another influential stereotype—or unsubstantiated position—this one expounded by Goldstein, Freud, and Solnit (1973) is that children need one home and one custodian, and that joint custody will lead to confusion and conflict in the child. In seeming support of this, the data suggest that paternal children were less manipulative with their parents than were joint children. Furthermore, there were cases in which the joint children were caught in the middle of parents making different rules. These data make clear the fact that a child cannot manipulate two parents if she or he is in contact with only one. Were Goldstein, Freud, and Solnit right all along?

It would be unreasonable to so conclude. In the first place, if the joint children in this sample had not been awarded to both parents, they would have been awarded to their mothers alone, and single mothers had the most difficult time disciplining.

Second, and more important, the testing and manipulating had all but disappeared by the time of the interview in each custody group. One must thus weigh the cost of temporarily enduring more manipulation against the advantages of joint disciplining. Those advantages are: (1) Joint parents do not feel overwhelmed because they have some time off; (2) joint parents have the benefit of the perspective of the other parent, which both single mothers and fathers missed; and (3) joint parents, in sharing disciplining after divorce, can continue to define their roles vis-à-vis their children as *parent* and not as indulging aunt or uncle.

It would seem that in the case of authority, as well as economics, joint custody at its best has advantages over single custody at its best.

5 Domestics

The results of this chapter are different from the hypothesized results. I predicted at the outset that divorced mothers would be taking for granted their domestic tasks and that *fathers* would be going mad trying to cook and keep house. What turned out to be the case was that both men and women ranked domestic responsibilities low on the Rank-Stress scale. And, for reasons to be explored, men had fewer problems than women in this area.

Change in Amount of Housework Performed

Single-Custody Mothers

One group of mothers (37 percent) reported that they were doing more housework at the time of the interview than they were before the divorce. Another 37 percent reported that they were doing *less* than before, and the remaining quarter reported no change. Those who reported doing more housework after the divorce explained that their husbands had shared the work during the marriage. The mothers doing less housework explained that working full time left them too tired to bother about housekeeping and that their priorities had changed as well:

> I work a fifty-hour week now. I don't have time to fuss over things like I used to. And then I realized it was a waste of time anyway. *What's wrong with a little dust?* I would rather relax when I come home. (Department store manager, son is fifteen.)

Said another mother, almost incredulous:

> I used to wash walls. And periodically I would take all the dishes out of the china cabinet and wash them! Now I work and go to graduate school and don't have time for that sort of thing. That used to be a big deal to have things sparkling clean when I was a housewife. I never liked doing it anyway. And now my life is so much more interesting. (Graduate student and secretary, children are sixteen and eighteen.)

Some women mentioned that housekeeping had been a bone of contention during the marriage:

99

He used to carry on almost every day about things being too messy. He
wanted the place to look like a museum, which is impossible with young
kids. It's a pleasure to set my own standards now, and that means cleaning
less. (Therapy aid, children are ten and fifteen.)

Although the mothers were not overwhelmed by the volume of cooking and
cleaning, many reported that they were doing many things that had not
previously entered into their definitions of housework. They were asked,
"What new things if any did you need to learn in order to keep up the
house?" Nearly all mothers answered "Many, many things!" or "I had to
learn everything!" Their comments on this question reveal an extreme
degree of isolation within the home during the marriage and in many cases
no familiarity with the world outside the home:

My God, I had to learn everything! To paint and check on the furnace.
Then the roof started leaking. I used to rely on my husband for all those big
things. Now I rely on my father a lot—and on myself! My son taught me to
fix the radiator hose. My girlfriends encouraged me to paint walls myself
since I knew how to paint ceramics. . . . I won't get on a thruway though. I
still go to see my father by taking the streets. Until a few years ago I
wouldn't make a left-hand turn; I'd go around and around. I'm afraid to
get out there—you know—get out there. (Avon representative, children are
ten, fifteen, and sixteen.)

Some women described themselves as Ibsen's Nora—having gone from
their father's keeping to their husband's and never having developed a sense
of self-sufficiency:

I had never even grocery shopped. He had owned a small store, and he
would bring home what we needed. The upkeep of the car was all new. I
was eighteen when I got married, and never had been alone, so at thirty-five
I was like an eighteen-year-old going out for the first time. Just paying rent
was a big deal. For two years I paid everything by money order because I
didn't know how to balance a checkbook. (Nurse's aid, children are eight,
ten, and sixteen.)

Another mother said that changing the storm windows was a "major ac-
complishment." She had confronted problems with plumbing and wiring in
the house and tried to keep the pool working. She felt completely overwhelmed at first because the divorce itself had been a crushing blow to her.
Here are her comments:

It was simply too many things to deal with at first, and I just wanted to die.
I had to calm myself, steady myself, and said: my first responsibility is to
the children. I would attend to them first. Then going to school myself
would be my second concern. I would take on the third thing—the

house—later. By then I was feeling better emotionally. I realized there are people you can call. You can call friends and repairmen. (Graduate student and secretary, children are sixteen and eighteen.)

While not all the women felt overwhelmed by their new responsibilities, each of them had a lengthy list of things they had had to face for the first time. This is in sharp contrast with the fathers' situations, which are discussed next.

Single-Custody Fathers

The domestic situation of the fathers was the inverse of the situation with the mothers. All the fathers were doing more housework at the time of the interview than they had prior to the divorce, but most did not feel that they had had to learn new tasks. Only half the fathers (compared with 87 percent of the mothers) had had to learn new domestic skills after the divorce. Fathers either had done such work during the marriage or had learned it before marrying. One-third of the fathers mentioned that they had had to expand their cooking repertoire but that nothing else was new. Only one-fourth of the fathers had had to learn a totally new skill. Even the descriptions of those fathers are nothing like the mothers', and their tone was much more matter-of-fact. When asked, "Did you have to learn anything new?" they responded:

No, everything had been shared during the marriage. It was fifty-fifty and we both cooked and did laundry and worked in the yard. So there was no unfamiliar territory—just more of it. It gets stressful. It would be nice to have someone to cook dinner for me sometimes. (Lawyer, sons are twelve and fourteen.)

One father's domestic credentials were quite impressive:

While married, I did the shopping and some housework and outside work. There is nothing new. Also I sew and crewl, and taught my daughter how. I was a short-order cook in the navy and do a lot of Chinese wok cooking now. It's the same as before—just more of it. (High school principal, children are twelve and fourteen.)

Some fathers said they had to expand their skills:

I was taught to cook when I was young, but I hadn't done much in seventeen years. So I had to learn to cook roasts and things. I experiment more with stuff. It was stressful at first to come home from work and then have to cook and straighten up the house. But after awhile you get into a routine. (Plumber, children are eight, thirteen, and fourteen.)

One-fourth of the fathers did have a lot to learn:

> I learned to be a woman. I cook now and wash clothes. That was no prob-
> lem. I even bake my own bread now because it's cheaper and better. It
> means staying on a very tight schedule though. Every single hour is planned
> out. (Toolmaker, children are eight and nine.)

Said another father:

> I wasn't completely helpless, but I had to learn to make a casserole. It's en-
> joyable now, although at first I felt taxed to the limit. I have an iron but
> rarely use it. We always look unironed. We have the natural look! (Physi-
> cian, son is thirteen.)

In contrast to the women who took very seriously their new tasks, the men
repeatedly expressed a casual attitude toward domestic demands:

> I had to relearn cooking and shopping. I don't care if it doesn't look like
> *Better Homes and Gardens.* We eat every meal off the grill in the backyard.
> (Business executive, daughter is seven.)

Said another man:

> We have a loose sort of thing. No way would I cook five meals a
> week—two maybe. A daughter will cook one meal per week. You saw how
> breakfast was. She (age seven) got herself a carrot and something else.
> We're terrible fridge-raiders. (College administrator, children are seven,
> fifteen, and sixteen.)

One father was especially articulate on this issue. His comments seem to
touch the root of the fathers' cavalier attitude about household labor:

> The things I didn't know how to do then—cooking and cleaning—I still
> don't know how to do. I get someone to do them for me. So I guess I have
> adjusted but not adapted! I don't worry. No matter how poor you are at
> those things, you're going to get by. You're not going to die if you don't
> know how to fix up the house. I'm sure I could have done more fixing up,
> and it would be neater and nicer here—but it wouldn't make any real dif-
> ference. We survive on pizza and sandwiches. Everyone is happy, and it's
> been five years. If I don't like to cook, I can't expect them to like it. I've
> never heard them complain. (Security guard, children are thirteen and
> fourteen.)

Indeed, the children of this father told me they enjoyed the casual norms
about eating in their house.

Only one father spoke in a baleful tone that echoed the mothers':

It's stressful, sure it is. To work all day and come home and have four little monsters sitting on the couch saying, "What are we having for dinner and when will it be ready?" It's rough. (Mechanic, children are four, eight, twelve, and thirteen.)

Contrary to expectation, most fathers were doing their domestic work themselves, and none had hired a housekeeper, although three fathers relied on their family for regular laundry or shopping. This leads into the question of which coping strategies parents used with regard to domestic labor.

Coping

The Mothers

In contrast to the findings of an earlier study (Brandwein, Brown, and Fox 1974), all the mothers in this sample reported having learned to do new tasks themselves. That is—they did not simply find someone else to do them. Who taught them how to fix radiators and remove storm windows?

Seventy percent reported that they counted on friends and lovers to help them with domestic tasks they could not manage. A few also mentioned parents, older children, and the landlord. Here are their comments:

My first objective is to learn how to do it myself. I found this book, *How to Fix Things in Your House,* and I consult it often. Some stuff like changing wiring is hard. I would ask friends to help me with that stuff. They would—you know—show me as they were doing it. My friends and I are really into sharing. (Unemployed mother, children are six and nine.)

Another mother mentioned that fixing things can involve the kids too:

I've had friends galore help me. The kids and I make a project out of it, and it's fun. Our last project was after Mike's foot went through Millie's window. We don't have enough money to spend every Saturday on the town, so we spend every Saturday doing fixing adventures together. (Student and secretary, children are seven, ten, and eleven.)

The active, rather than passive approach that these mothers have taken toward domestic problems augurs a positive outcome, according to crisis theory. Jens defined adaptive coping in this way:

Coping is adaptive when, as a result of the experience, a person changes his coping schemes in such a way that he is better prepared to cope with future difficult events, i.e. his repertoire of coping responses is broadened and better organized.[1]

Another way of reorganizing domestic work is to involve children in it. Parents were asked, "Do you enlist the children to help you more since the divorce?" Nearly all mothers had their children doing more housework since the divorce to compensate for their father's absence. This typically meant doing more dishes and cleaning as well as some cooking and laundry. Mothers tended to see this help as very important. Here is an account of an extreme case:

> My daughter, Heather, has done all the housework since she was thirteen. Sometimes I have felt guilty and have told her not to do so much, but she says, "If I don't do it, it won't get dome." I think she takes out her frustrations in that way. I could never have raised these kids without her help. (Nurse's aid, children are eight, ten, and sixteen.)

Almost all the mothers felt comfortable making more demands on their children. They explained that the children sometimes complained but that they did their work fairly faithfully:

> They hate cleaning just like I do. But I say—we all live her. We all make it dirty. We all clean it up. No way do I feel guilty about it—no way! (Unemployed mother, children are six and nine.)

Only two mothers had reservations about placing more responsibility on their children:

> No, the kids don't do any more than before. I have tried to keep things as normal as possible—as much the way they were as possible. I don't want to ask any more of them. They have been through enough. (Unemployed librarian, children are eleven, thirteen, and fourteen.)

The Fathers

Only half of the fathers had enlisted their children in more domestic work than before the divorce. There were a variety of reasons why fathers did not demand regular chores of their children:

> It would be good for him to be helping more with the house, I think. And I know it would be better for me! But I wanted to keep everything as normal as possible. I do it all—all the meals and the laundry; I even make his lunch although he's capable of making his own. His mother did those things for him. (Physician, son is thirteen.)

Said another father:

> I feel guilty about making them help. I say—"I know it isn't your fault that there is only one parent to do the work. I got you into this. But we have to

make a go of it." (High school principal, children are twelve and fourteen.)

This sex difference is consistent with the information that emerged from the
authority chapter. Recall that mothers tend to make more rules and become
firmer and that fathers tend to relax their authority after divorce. There was
also some suggestion that fathers wanted to feel more like peers with their
children.

Fathers were similar to mothers in that they too actively solicited help
with domestic tasks from people besides their children. Each father cited
either a family member or friend who had taken time to show him
something. Here are some typical comments:

> I'm adventurous and just started following recipes. I dated one girl who
> gave me a lot of pointers. Her mother bought me a cookbook for
> Christmas. I'm good at asking people for help. I would ask my mother, for
> example. (Toolmaker, children are eight and nine.)

Said another man:

> Ladies in laundromats are more than willing to flirt with you and show you
> how to do it. (Psychiatrist, children are fifteen and seventeen.)

Nineteen percent of fathers were receiving direct help from relatives.
For example, the parents of one father did his grocery shopping for him
weekly because they are retired and enjoy helping out. Another father said
that his sister had been doing his laundry for seven years. Still another
father said that for the first year after the divorce, he and his daughter ate
three meals a day at his mother's house. There were no mothers who had
this type of routine assistance. It is not clear whether the mothers simply
were not offered this type of help or whether they turned it down. One
possibility is that friends and family tend to feel sorry for a lone father and
step in to help more often.

Advantages

Parents were asked, "Are there any advantages to being solely responsible
for domestic work?"

The Fathers

It is logical that because the fathers had less to learn than the mothers, they
would see fewer advantages in being the sole head of housekeeping. Fathers

in fact reported that there were no real advantages. Only a few said that "I like being domestic" or "I can do my own thing now. It's really all my house."

The Mothers

Over half the mothers cited advantages to being totally responsible for domestics. Typical comments ran as follows:

> I feel really good that we've survived and have done a good job of it. It's fine for women to be independent. My mother is completely helpless. I never would have learned how competent I can be if it weren't for the divorce. (Unemployed mother, children are thirteen and fourteen.)

Said another woman:

> If I ever enter another relationship, it will be because I really want to—and not just to have someone to lean on—because I can stand on my own two feet now! (Nurse's aid, children are eight, ten, and sixteen.)

Again, the difference between mothers and fathers on this issue can be explained by certain tenets of crisis theory. Crisis theory says that the new equilibrium reached after the crisis can leave the organism at a level of functioning either higher or lower than before the crisis. An important determinant of that new level of functioning is the type of coping strategy used by the individual. What makes a coping strategy effective? According to Jens's review of the literature, the best coping strategies are "flexible" and "reality oriented." *Flexibility* here means that the coper does not rely rigidly on one method alone and is able to give up the method when it is no longer useful. *Reality orientation* means task orientation and refers to methods that are problem solving in nature rather than merely anxiety reducing (for example, learning to change a fuse as opposed to crying or drinking to relieve tension.)

It seems clear that the mothers in the study were coping in flexible and task-oriented ways, and it is clear that most felt they were functioning at a higher level than they had before the divorce. The fathers, however, had not experienced a crisis in this area in the first place so they did not have the necessity or the opportunity to grow from it.

Joint Custody and Domestics

Like single mothers and fathers, joint parents ranked domestic work low on the Rank-Stress scale. Their attitudes are isomorphic with those of the single-custody parents. They will be described briefly below.

Significantly more joint mothers than single mothers had cut back on housework since the divorce. This may be because twice as many joint as single mothers are professionals (66 percent versus 31 percent) whose lives are made more hectic by meetings, and so on. Another factor is that the joint children on the average were younger than the singles' children (ten years versus twelve years) and that joint mothers thus had demands that took them away from housework.

As for joint fathers—two-thirds reported that they were doing more housework than before. This is similar to the single fathers' response (75 percent).

New Tasks

The Mothers. Almost all the joint mothers, like the single-custody mothers, had to learn new things in order to run the household alone. Again, those tasks included fixing appliances, repairing cars, hanging pictures, and so on. All women felt that learning these things was both stressful and exciting. Here is a typical comment:

> He was good about repairing things. Now I hang pictures, drill holes, and even stripped the floor. Once I even fixed my drier. I just took off the back and saw what was wrong with it. It was maddening at first. I didn't even own a screwdriver. I had never put gas in the car before. (Joint mother, student and waitress, children are five, nine, and twelve.)

It is interesting also to note the exception, however, where the roles were reversed:

> I always did the repairing. My husband said when his wife left, he lost an electrician, a plumber, and a TV repairman. (Joint mother, unemployed, children are eleven and twelve, split week.)

The Fathers. Nearly half of the joint fathers said they had nothing new to learn because they had helped out during the marriage. However, half cited cooking as new, and one cited the organizing and coordinating of the household that his ex had done previously:

> I was unaware of how much invisible planning is needed in running a house. My wife had always done those things—keeping track of what we ran out of, making appointments, and so on. The first time I went on vacation alone, I left in a mad rush. She had always organized things like that. (Joint father, lawyer, children are four and fourteen, split week.)

Coping

Joint mothers reported that they simply "plunged in" to their new tasks. Two mothers mentioned counting on friends to do things and teach them how. One mother was still relying on her ex-husband for assistance:

> He hooked up my washer and dryer and will hang a picture. He'll fix the car and teach me how. I hate being dependent on him, but I can't afford to pay someone to do it. (Joint mother, student, children are four and fourteen, split week.)

Only two of the joint mothers reported that their children were doing more housework since the divorce. They said they were demanding more because the children were older and because their help was needed more. Only one mother felt guilty about the children's doing more work:

> I feel mostly bad about their doing more. If I was a good mother—or if the divorce hadn't happened—they wouldn't be doing this. (Joint mother Z, student and waitress, children are five, nine, and twelve.)

Over half the joint fathers said their children were doing more work. Fathers did not feel guilty about it because they felt it encouraged independence.

Advantages

As was the case with single custodians, two-thirds of joint mothers cited advantages to being head of the household. They mentioned the gratification of mastering new tasks and the freedom of living in a space you alone control:

> There is a tremendous feeling of space and freedom. I only have myself to please. And it's great to feel—if the radiator breaks, so what? I'm competent; I can fix it. (Joint mother, social worker, children are six, seven, nine, ten, and twelve, children split week.)

Conclusions: Solo Parenting in the Space Age

Contrary to expectation, women had more problems with domestic responsibilities than men did essentially because women faced more unfamiliar tasks.

The fathers' accounts were dispassionate. It was not the case that single parenthood found them frantically burning pancakes or shrinking clothes in the dryer. Nor had these fathers hired housekeepers as substitute wives.

Comical images of men as domestically helpless do not conform to the men in this study. Probably those images come from the many television situation comedies about single fathers of the 1950s and 60s. (Some of those shows were *"Andy Griffith," "My Three Sons," "Family Affair," "Bachelor Father,"* and *"The Courtship of Eddy's Father."*) In contrast to the fathers in this study, all of those television fathers had a *live-in* housekeeper. (Interestingly, shows about single mothers, for example, *"Julia"* and *"The Partridge Family"*, did not have housekeepers.) The question posed in this essay is—why could fathers in the study do what Fred McMurray couldn't?

The most fundamental difference has to do with the change in technology from 1950 to 1980. It would have been tougher to do domestic tasks alone thirty years ago (and an extraordinary burden to have done this in earlier epochs). The availability for mass consumption of washers and dryers as well as disposable diapers, permanent-press clothing, fast and frozen foods, crock-pots and microwave ovens means that learning to do housework is in fact now a fairly trivial process. Some parents mentioned this fact in the interview; most took it for granted.

If one has any doubt about the importance of this technology in actually shaping family functions and structures, one need only turn to the underdeveloped world for illustrations. In Cuba, for example, the absence of advanced technology has impeded progress toward the national goal of equalizing the social position of women and men—both within the family and beyond. In formulating social change in this area, Cubans considered domestic labor to be very important because it has historically meant a "double shift" for women working outside the home. Thus the revised Family Code (1976) stipulates that husbands and wives must share domestic work fifty-fifty. (This section of the law is read into the marriage ceremony.) Implementing this practice has not been simple—for a host of reasons. In the summer of 1979, I spent many hours talking with Cuban women about housework. They said that even the most radical men who applauded the new law had trouble learning to iron and sew. Ironing involves learning not only the physical skill but also the properties of different fabrics. Clothing is scarce in Cuba so mending clothes and altering hand-me-downs become important tasks. The shortages caused by the embargo make all work more tedious. For example, grocery shopping is not a thirty-five-minute relay through Super Duper; it is a two-hour wait in a meat-ration line—and then another line. Many women said it was easier to "do it myself" than to teach the men—or in some cases, to cajole the men—into doing housework. These lags in technology contribute to the fact that only 28 percent of Cuban women are employed outside the home (Castro 1974). For economic reasons, the government would like this figure to be much higher. And, after divorce, women almost always get custody of children. (The domestic burden on men is not the only reason for this, of course.)

In the United States, technological innovations have made it easy for men to learn "women's work"—but not vice versa. There are no quick, automated solutions for changing storm windows or repairing roofs. The tasks the mothers had to learn involved more complex skills, more danger, and greater expense. No wonder that they struggled more than fathers over these tasks and that they also felt more gratified having mastered them.

Technological change, however, cannot alone account for the results of this chapter. Note that fathers did not say only that housekeeping was "easy"—they also said that it was not important. The mothers said the same thing. Not only were they too tired to clean but they had also changed their minds about the *value of cleaning.* I would argue that this change in attitude toward domestic labor is a product of the women's movement and that it is almost as important as the technological advance. Betty Friedan in *The Feminine Mystique* "demystified" housework to the point that it seemed like "indoor loitering."[2] Since that time the women's movement has been seriously concerned with housework—with its role in the economy, its relationship to women's depression, and so on (see Mainardi 1970). This concern has translated into an exhortation: to share housework, to discuss the oppressiveness of the "squeaky-clean" standard with fellow toilers, and in general to allow it to interfere as little as possible with the real business of one's life. (Recall the ubiquitous "Fuck Housework" poster of the 1970s.)

Without this important change in the superstructure, the changes in "hardware" would not have had their full impact on society. This attitudinal change is reflected in the account of the graduate student and secretary whose former habit of cleaning dishes in the china cabinet now seemed to her like a fetish. Attitudinal change is apparent also in the security guard father who fairly boasted that his children lived on pizza and sandwiches and who did no cleaning at all.

Bachelor Father would have had to make a better show of it.

Notes

1. K. Field Jens, "Studies of the Coping Process: A Review" (Unpublished manuscript, 1976), p. 8. Department of Psychology, State University of New York at Buffalo.

2. B. Ehrenreich, "How to Get Housework out of Your System," *Ms.* 8 (1979):47-80.

6 Child Care

Becoming the Primary Caretaker

All the single-custody mothers and fathers felt more and not less competent as parents since the divorce. The reason was that they felt happier and "better adjusted" than during the marriage. I took special notice of the five fathers who acquired custody of children who were four years or younger at the time. Men are not socialized to be primary caretakers of children. Caring alone for infants, one might assume, would be particularly intimidating.

I asked one father, "When you got custody of Cookie and Greg, they were sixteen months and two and a half years old. Did that seem awesome?" He answered:

> Yeah, I was scared to death. I had taken care of them a little bit while we were married. Like I would change a diaper—but not a messy diaper. I just decided I had to do it. Their mother neglected them, and I was worried to death while they were in her custody. When she called and asked if I wanted them, I knew I had to say yes without even thinking about it. Teen sitters didn't work well with them at that age, so I took them to people's houses while I worked—to women with children of their own. In some cases it worked out OK, but in some cases they were looked down upon as foster children. Then I got Mrs. Mack—a sixty-year-old woman who took care of them real good. She only stayed six months and then moved. She said I didn't do a bad job of diapering. . . . It's true that they have had a huge number of different sitters in their lives—but that has its good side too. We all like meeting new people. . . . (Toolmaker, children are eight and nine.)

A father who attained custody of four girls who were two to eleven-years old at the time said:

> Sure I was scared. Maggie was just a baby then. There were times I thought I was going to wake up and this was all a dream. It was nice coming home knowing my wife was taking care of them. But we've managed. . . . The fact is that no matter how much I holler, or how awful I cook—they're still better off with me because I love them, and I ain't going nowhere. (Mechanic, daughters are four, eight, twelve, and thirteen.)

A third father said he would have been apprehensive were it not for the presence of his lover who adores the children and who took a lot of responsibility for them. There were two fathers, however, who did not feel panic—even initially:

> I had no predeliction *not* to care for babies. I have never felt that mothering was the peculiar domain of mothers. When we split, he had been weaned; of course, *that* is the peculiar domain of mothers! But I felt no less inclined to toilet train him, teach him to talk or love him and hug him and stay up when he was sick than any mother I know. And clearly I was more inclined toward these things than his own mother because she wanted Josh and I to stay tcgether while she went to follow her work. (Professor, son is seven.)

Said another father:

> No, I wasn't scared to have custody. I was scared when he was with her. She wasn't stable—she had a lot of problems. You don't have to be a woman to raise a child. If you're getting at some maternal instinct—I don't know. I think I have more of it than she does. It would be great for Bobby as well as for me if I remarry because we both need company. But it's not that I'm looking for a mommy for him. (Architect, son is three.)

It is important to note that the ex-wives of all three of these fathers were out of town, and those of the other two visited the children only sporadically. Thus these fathers definitely were parenting without the help of the children's mothers.

Substitute Care

One thing that single parenthood brings to almost all parents of young children is the need for more substitute care. Whereas during marriage a couple might go out once a week or less, the single parent often dates three times per week. Also, while a married parent can attend a meeting and leave the children with the other parent, the single parent must hire a sitter.

Even more basic to the lives of these children is the fact that many of them spent more time in substitute *daytime* care than before the divorce. (Approximately one-third of the parents in each custody group reported more use of daytime care because of the divorce.) The reason for this is that, if not for the divorce, the child's mother would have been home full time or at least part time.

Just how much substitute care have these children had in their lives? Table 6-1 shows the percentage of children within each custody type who have experienced substitute daytime care. Mothers, fathers, and joint parents utilized approximately the same amount of substitute care. Roughly half the children in each custody type had been placed in some type of daytime care. The largest number of children were placed in the care of a

Table 6-1
Percentage of Children in Each Custody Type who Have Experienced
Substitute Care

| Amount of Substitute Care | Custody Type[a] (n = Number of Children in the Type) | | |
	Maternal (34)	Paternal (32)	Joint (25)
20-40 hours per week	29%	37%	32%
10-19 hours per week	23%	9%	24%
Total percentage of children who have been in substitute care	52%	46%	56%

[a]Responses of the fathers and joint parents did not differ significantly from those of the single mothers. $X^2(2) = 3.5; p > .05$.

babysitter. Daycare centers were the second most popular. Other children were placed in the care of a family member or lover.

The utilization of more substitute care naturally brings its own set of problems and advantages. The problem will be discussed next.

Problems of Using More Substitute Care

The Mothers. Of the mothers who worked after the divorce and who had young children, 75 percent reported that the availability of affordable care had been, or continued to be, a major problem in their lives. They tried a variety of solutions to this obstacle—each with its own set of problems. Here is the account of a mother with a high school education who had been working as a pharmacist's assistant:

> I made $90 per week and paid $50 per week to the sitter. I had money left for food and that was it. There has never been a daycare center convenient for me, no matter where I've lived. Or else it had age and time limits. Please put this in your report. *We need daycare.* Working mothers more than anyone else. We need some responsible people to watch our children so we can go out and work and get off welfare. (Unemployed mother, children are six and nine.)

The problem described by this mother was by no means limited to women in the lower education bracket. Here is the account of a mother with a B.A.:

> The cost of childcare was a horrendous problem when they were little. I earned only $10 a week during the summer after sitters were paid, but I

had to maintain that job in order to make money during the winter when they were in school. (Paralegal, children are ten, fourteen, and sixteen.)

One solution to the dilemma was to use extended family members as sitters:

On my salary I can't afford daycare. The consequence is that I rely on my mother more than I would like. The problem is that she is not good with Kenny; they don't get along. I try to get a sitter whenever I can afford it. (LPN, children are four and eight.)

Two mothers were forced to move in with their parents precisely because they could not afford childcare. The account of one of these women appeared in chapter 3. She described the problems of trying to discipline a four-year-old in the presence of indulging grandparents. The other mother moved in with her parents for six months during a Buffalo winter which, she said, "felt like twenty-seven years." She and her parents had never had a close relationship. That fact, along with the frustrations of living in cramped quarters, resulted in acting out on the part of her four- and seven-year-old children. The children's problems abated when they moved out of the grandparents' house.

The Fathers. Several men cited the cost of childcare as a disadvantage, but only one father described it as a major problem. This was the toolmaker who works second shift six days per week and who must hire sitters to stay with his eight and nine year olds for this entire time—that is, from 2:30 P.M. until midnight. He relies on teenage sitters who live in the area, some of whom are mature and competent, others of whom are not. He would love to have daycare available. It would mean fewer scheduling headaches and less turnover for the children, but there is no daycare center that offers evening hours.

Joint-Custody Families. Fewer joint parents than single parents utilized substitute evening care (table 6-2). In fact, a number of joint families (36 percent) reported that when their children were younger, they relied on (or still do rely on) their ex-spouse exclusively for substitute care. These parents explained that they did their partying, dating, and errands when the children were with their ex-spouse. In joint-custody families this constitutes a large and regular chunk of time, in contrast to the time the visiting parent spends with the child. Joint parents felt that this set-up was optimal because the children could spend time with the other parent who loved and needed them, as opposed to being with a "stranger." This strategy is also more convenient and less expensive. All four sets of parents explained that this worked out comfortably:

Table 6-2
Percentage of Parents Using More Substitute Care after Divorce than before

	Custodian[a] (n)		
	Mothers (16)	Fathers (16)	Joint Parents (11)
More evening care	62%	68%	36%
More daytime care	31%	31%	36%

[a]Significantly fewer joint parents than single-custody parents use more substitute evening care. $X^2(1) = 3.84; p = 0.05$.

> In three years since the separation, I have never hired a sitter. I don't date on the nights they're here because I want to be with them. And there is plenty of time for me to do that. If something unusual comes up in my schedule, I know that they can go with their father—and he knows the same. (Joint mother C, real-estate agent, children are nine and ten, split day.)

No single-custody parent reported having this arrangement. There is thus some suggestion that joint parents have it easier when it comes to childcare. The more equally the time is shared, the more likely this arrangement becomes. In cases where children split the year or alternate years, this substitute-care arrangement is clearly infeasible. In the four cases just mentioned, children split the week or the day between parents who lived fifteen to twenty minutes away from each other.

Quality of Substitute Care

A few mothers and fathers expressed concern about the quality of care their children received from sitters. One of them was the mother of a child with a birth defect that makes caring for him difficult. Most parents felt comfortable with the quality of care their children received, and some even believed it was a marvelous opportunity for growth for their children. One mother described her daughter's daycare center in this way:

> They are really wonderful. For example, one day they had a "men's morning" instead of fathers' morning, and one of my friends went with her. They are very sophisticated there. They did a unit on families, and they showed pictures of one-parent families too. On career day they brought in physicians who were women. . . . I feel lucky that she's in that environment. (Assistant professor, daughter is seven.)

Among the joint-custody families, only one joint mother was deeply concerned about the quality of substitute care her children receive when they are with their father. In this family children live with their father on a farm and stay with mother every other weekend in the city. They have a sitter come in the morning to get them off to school and to care for them in the evening and make dinner. Mother described the problem as follows:

> He lives out too far, and it doesn't pay much. There are five kids, and he wants the sitter to cook and clean. So there is a very high turnover, and the kids complain. We had a very good older woman who would sit and hold the kids, but her husband wouldn't let her work. (Joint mother X, social worker, children are six, seven, nine, ten, and twelve, split week.)

Because this mother is a social worker, she had an interesting comment about childcare in general:

> We need grandmother types who will come into the home and take care of children. We need loving people. It's a shame too because we have displaced homemakers—women who are out in the world for the first time in thirty years with no "job skills." Well, if those women have been in the home for thirty years, they are not without skills, and they're just what we need. Instead, we have training classes for displaced homemakers at the YWCA, while single parents cry out for help.

Contact and Closeness with Children

Parents were asked if they felt they had more or less contact with their children since the divorce than during the marriage.

The Mothers

Half the mothers reported that they had less contact with their children than before the divorce; about one third felt they had more, and the remainder said it was the same. Several mothers were unhappy about spending less time with their children because of having to work. A typical comment was:

> I'd rather be here when they get home from school, and I miss baking for them. I think of a mother baking when kids come home. I do less with them now because I work and go out on dates. (Nurse's aid, daughters are eight, ten, and sixteen.)

The mothers who were spending more time with their children commented, for example:

I spend more time with them now. I have to. It's important for them to have me around because they have no one else. And I enjoy that time now because I'm a happier person. When I was married, I was depressed and hassled and didn't enjoy my children. (Student and secretary, children are seven, ten, and eleven.)

Indeed, despite the fact that some mothers were spending less time with their children, 100 percent of mothers felt they had maintained the same level of closeness with their children as before the divorce—or that they had grown even closer. The reasons for this closeness centered on the same themes: first, that mother was a happier person and therefore more able to enjoy living and parenting. Second was the fact that they and their children had "been through a lot together" as they struggled to make ends meet, to help each other through sad days, and as they tried to fix the washer together. The third reason was, "the kids need me more than before"—because father was no longer on the scene.

The Fathers

The situation with fathers looked different. Eighty-seven percent of single fathers were spending more time with their children than before the divorce; 6 percent said less, and 6 percent said it had not changed. These data make sense because while the mothers were comparing the present to the time they had been home constantly with the children, fathers were comparing the present with the time when they saw their children only on returning home at night.

Fathers, like mothers, felt as close or closer to their children after divorce. Here is a typical comment:

I have more contact with them now. I used to go to every meeting I could think of to be away from the house. I enjoy being with the kids now. (Lawyer, sons are twelve and fourteen.)

Joint-Custody Mothers

The situation with joint mothers is slightly different from that of single mothers. All joint mothers reported less contact with their children than before the divorce. Only one-third of these mothers felt unequivocally good about the amount of contact they presently had with their children. Some comments from the mothers with mixed feelings follow:

I'm frustrated about having less contact with them. I have to do an incredible amount of juggling: time for myself, for kids, social activities, and so on. I miss them when they're not here. (Joint mother A, doctoral student, children are six and twelve, split week.)

Said another mother:

I see them less because I work now and go to school and they spend part of the week with their father. In the beginning it bothered me a lot. I'm getting used to it now. I feel—that's life. (Joint mother Z, student and waitress, children are five, nine, and twelve, split week.)

Only one joint mother desired actually to change the situation. She is mother Z, just quoted, whose family was categorized earlier as problematic. She would like to cut out visitation with the father completely.

One joint mother said point blank that her relationship with her children had suffered because she did not have full custody:

I knew that once they stayed with their father, there would be a campaign against me. He and his mother have poisoned the kids against me. They spend more time with him, and he uses that time to brainwash them. I don't know if I'll ever be as close to them as before. (Joint mother Y, unemployed, children are eleven and twelve, split week.)

The other two mothers spoke of mixed feelings:

I feel less close to them because I don't see them daily. But I feel closer to them because I'm the only one here. The closeness and confidence aren't diffused when they're here. (Joint mother A, doctoral student, sons are six and twelve, split week.)

All the other mothers felt their relationship with the children had been maintained at *least* at the predivorce level. Here is one mother's insight:

Divorce is a major trauma. You become more aware of the tenuousness of human relationships. And you realize that your children won't be with you forever. So the time we have together feels special, and we're definitely closer. (Joint mother D, research assistant, children are twelve and fourteen, split week.)

Joint-Custody Fathers

As was the case with single fathers, joint fathers spoke of having "taken for granted" their child-care responsibilities during the marriage. Each of the joint fathers felt comfortable with the amount of contact they had. None felt resigned or guilty about it. All felt that they had either increased or maintained their predivorce level of closeness with the children. Here is a typical comment:

I spend more time than before. It's special time. Not that it's all out on the town, but we horse around more. I feel close to them and don't know exactly why. It has to do with dealing with them on a one-to-one basis and not as part of a family. It's an uncluttered relationship. (Joint father A, physicist, children are six and twelve, split week.)

The Cost of Closeness

We have established that the sheer amount of time spent with children increased for the majority of parents in the sample and that most parents felt as close or closer to their children than previously. This reality naturally raises the question, "Does all that closeness ever feel stifling?" The point was to find out if single parents sometimes felt the need to create distance from their children.

The majority of single-custody mothers and fathers responded that there were indeed times when proximity with their children seemed excessive. Some felt resigned to this feeling. Others described ways they had discovered to cope with this problem—mainly through the use of the extended family. (This is discussed again in the next chapter.) Here are some representative comments:

When they were younger, they would just filter back and forth into my sister's house who lived nearby. When I needed peace, I could send them there and she could do the same. For dinner—at times I would have two children, and sometimes five. It was wonderful—for them to get away too. (Paralegal, children are ten, fourteen, and sixteen.)

Said another mother:

I'm lucky. I have friends who will take my daughter when I don't feel well, or need to get some work done and want to be alone. (Assistant professor, daughter is seven.)

Another mother commented—only half in jest:

I love my kids, but I'm with them twenty-four hours a day, seven days a week, three hundred sixty-five days a year. . . . They should have a summer camp for mothers! (Unemployed mother, daughters are thirteen and fourteen.)

I could not resist informing the mother just quoted that in Sweden, mothers are entitled to state-funded vacations for psychological renewal![1]

Joint parents do seem to have the advantage in making substitute child-care arrangements. Without asking for it, without imposing on anyone or

paying anyone, they have regular breaks from parenting. Only one joint
father reported feeling overwhelmed with childcare. This was Mr. F, whose
children do not go to live with their mother until summer.

Conclusions

Dissolution of the marital dyad almost always leads to more substitute care
for children. This was true of the families in this study and is true for the
population of divorced parents in general.[2] Although some of the parents in
the sample mentioned that they preferred extended family members over
daycare centers, there was a general acceptance of daycare as an option.
Some parents, in fact, felt that their children really benefited from the
stimulation of the daycare center and that they learned good social skills
from so much interaction with peers. This represents a major attitude
change from thirty years ago. Dr. Spock warned for decades that maternal
employment led to child neglect. An Expert Committee of the World Health
Organization, moreover, concluded that the use of daycare produced "permanent damage to the emotional health of a future generation."[3] A 1980
review of the literature concludes, however, that no one has been able to
demonstrate deleterious effects of maternal employment or daycare on
children.[4]

While attitudes—both professional and lay—have changed on the subject of daycare, resources do not exist to begin to fill the demand. Here is an
important illustration of the larger society failing to support family needs.
The dearth of daycare programs in the United States makes childcare a terrible burden for the divorced family. Once again, the problem is more
serious for single mothers than fathers because of money. In some cases, the
cost of daycare is equivalent to a woman's salary. In Buffalo, for example,
the least expensive daycare at the time of the interview was $2,000 per year
per child. Recall that most mothers had two children, and that their median
income was $4,000-$9,000. At least one woman in the study had stopped
working altogether because she could not afford child care. She was a very
intelligent and ambitious woman and was deeply unhappy about having to
"retire from the outside world."

Because of population trends, the number of preschool children in the
country will be 36 percent greater in 1990 than in 1977. Children of working
mothers will have increased 63 percent by then.[5] The demand for daycare is
thus bound to increase in the next two decades; however, state and federal
human-services budgets do not currently give sufficient priority to child
care. Single parents may start their own child-care collectives to fill the gap.
Perhaps more parents will opt for joint custody because of the advantage it
offers in the area of child care (that is, parents rely on each other for child
care).

The notion that substitute care is psychologically damaging to children has probably contributed to the belief that the postdivorce family is a "broken" family or "nonfamily." As late as 1978 a Supreme Court Justice wrote, "Divorce dissolves the family as well as the marriage, a reality that may not be ignored."[6] Behind such despairing statements often lurks a horror of children being raised by "strangers" while their mothers work.

The families in this study were families, without a doubt. All parents felt more and not less competent as parents. The majority of fathers were spending more time with the children than before the divorce, and the majority of all parents felt as close or closer to the children than during the marriage. When this closeness became excessive, parents coped by allowing the children to spend more time with family and friends. Thus there is the possibility of the divorced family transforming itself into a unit with a greater, and not narrower, network of support. This issue of support systems before and after divorce is addressed at length in the next chapter.

Notes

1. Swedish Institute, *Social Benefits in Sweden* (Stockholm: Trygg Hansa, 1977).

2. C. Etaugh, "Effects of Nonmaternal Care on Children," *American Psychologist* 35 (1980):309-319.

3. World Health Organization (WHO) Expert Committee on Mental Health, Report of the Second Session, Technical Report Series No. 31, WHO Monograph, Geneva, 1951.

4. Etaugh, "Effects of Nonmaternal Care."

5. S. Hofferth, Daycare in the Next Decade: 1980-1990," *Journal of Marriage and the Family*, August 1979, pp. 649-657.

6. *Braiman* v. *Braiman,* 44 N.Y. 2nd 584, 407 N.Y.S. 2nd 449, 378 N.E. 2nd 1019 (1978).

7 Support Systems

Loneliness: Single-Custody Mothers and Fathers

Single fathers ranked "loneliness" as number 1 on the Rank-Stress scale. Mothers ranked it as number 3. A section of the interview was devoted to exploration of this issue to determine how parents constructed a support system to cope with loneliness.

It is essential to note that loneliness was not a new problem—a sudden change caused by the divorce. Some people actually felt less lonely since the divorce, although this did not alter the fact that it was still a major life problem—"like the diffference between a third-degree and a second-degree burn," as one mother said. Robert Weiss's well-known work with the newly separated revealed that separated men and women suffer fear, anxiety, and panic in the early stages of separation—regardless of how unsatisfactory the marriage had been.[1] Weiss has suggested that the persisting bond between spouses resembles the attachment bond of children to their parents, as described by Bowlby.[2] The parents in this study were *not* newly separated; they had been apart from their spouse for 3.5 years on the average. Their descriptions of loneliness therefore do not resemble those of Weiss's informants in emotional intensity.

When asked why they felt lonely, men and women gave the same kinds of answers, for example, having to break the habit of a constant companion and shouldering the responsibility of raising children alone. Here are some comments from the single-custody mothers:

> It is very real. When you have lived with someone a long time, you are used to that comfort. I miss the arm around me and having someone always there. And there were times when the marriage was good. (Graduate student and secretary, children are sixteen and eighteen.)

Said another woman:

> I'm a very sexual person, and suddenly I realized, hey! What will I do for sex? (Unemployed mother, children are six and nine.)

Another typical comment was:

> I checked loneliness as number 1, not because of emotional reasons but because of the responsibilities. My lover can't share all the problems of the

children or the financial problems. I feel that I am single with married responsibilities. (LPN, children are four and eight.)

The fathers' accounts touched the same themes:

You asked me what it was like suddenly having five kids alone. I didn't think of it like that. The only thing on my mind was—what am *I* doing here alone? I felt abandoned. (College administrator, children are seven, fifteen, and sixteen.)

Another father said:

Loneliness is a problem; that's why I stayed in the marriage so long. The day-to-day hassles of caring for kids can be outasite. (Computer programmer, children are ten and fourteen.)

The Support Group

What do single-custody parents do about their loneliness? Informants were asked to describe their support group as it was at the time of the interview and as it was before the divorce. *Support group* was defined for them as "the people you count on most for love, and for help of any kind—for example, financial help, babysitting, repairs, and confiding problems."

One clear result that emerged from the interviews was that the support systems of both mothers and fathers changed dramatically after the divorce. Table 7-1 shows that 62 percent of mothers and fathers reported that there was *no overlap* between their support group of the present and that of the predivorce past! Only one mother said her support network was essentially the same as before. Why should this transformation in support structure occur? Respondents cited a variety of reasons. Approximately one-third of the mothers and one-third of the fathers explained that during the marriage, their

Table 7-1
Percentage of Parents Who Felt There Was Overlap between Their Pre- and Postdivorce Support Groups

	Custodian (n)			
Amount of Overlap	Mothers (16)	Fathers (16)	Joint Mothers (9)	Joint Fathers (9)
Complete	6%	—	11%	—
Partial	31%	37%	23%	34%
None	62%	62%	66%	66%

spouse had been their support group; that is, they had lived lives insulated from activities and people. Here is an example:

> My husband was my support group before the divorce. He didn't like to go out much, and he wouldn't allow me to go out with my girl friends. He wanted me always home—and I just got comfortable living that way. I leaned on him for everything. (Therapy aid, children are ten and fifteen.)

Other parents said that they had changed friends after the divorce because they felt so changed by the experience that the old friends had nothing in common with them:

> There are people with whom I was very close who are not part of my life at all now. We'll chat in the grocery store—but that's all. A lot of them are interested in recipes and soap operas—and that just isn't my life any more. I am going to school and working and meeting stimulating people. (Graduate student and secretary, children are sixteen and eighteen.)

Still other parents mentioned that their friends had stopped contacting them:

> Some friends drifted away from me. Single people have different needs and interests than married people. Also, friends sometimes don't want to take sides. (Machinist, children are eleven, twelve, and fourteen.)

Said another father:

> I've lost some friends through the process of divorce. I withdrew from various people as part of my own adjusting, part of becoming a single person. (Physician, son is thirteen.)

These accounts do not seem emotional. Parents seemed to view breaking away from certain friends as part of breaking away from their spouse and starting a new life. Again, these interviews took place 3.5 years after the break-up, so much of the pain had already dissolved.

Beyond the replacement of married friends with new single friends, the postdivorce support systems are broader than the predivorce support systems. As mentioned earlier, a fair number of parents reported that during the marriage, their spouse had been their support group. Only a few parents cited their own parents or friends or therapists as important members of their predivorce support group. In contrast, the postdivorce support groups include: parents, neighbors, siblings, the children themselves, singles' groups, colleagues, therapists, ministers, lovers, and lawyers. The most often-named supports were parents and singles' groups—perhaps dividing in two the role of the ex-spouse (that is, providing assistance and love on the one hand and companionship and sex on the other).

Singles Groups

Exactly half the mothers and half the fathers named a singles group as part of their support network [for example, Parents Without Partners (PWP); Common Dimensions, Inc., (CDI); Time And Place (TAP); Fathers for Equal Rights; and MOMMA.] Here are some comments about these groups:

> Now most of my emotional support comes from male friends who are also single. We met through PWP. I don't like the bar scene, so I go to PWP to meet women. What I attend most often is the discussion groups. We discuss all kinds of things—a certain book or what loneliness means or raising children alone. Also my son attends a lot of their functions, and he loves it. (Salesman, son is thirteen.)

A mother who had established the local chapter of MOMMA described the organization:

> MOMMA tries to respond to the needs women have other than dating—that is, information and support about the divorce process itself, about lawyers, rights, money, and jobs. Women are in no way prepared to go through divorce. There are people in my group I can really count on to talk over a problem. (Secretary, son is four.)

MOMMA has since changed its name to "Single-Parentscope" and now includes both men and women.

It is clear that there exists in the urban United States and entire "singles subculture." Only 12 percent of all the single-custody parents had never attended a meeting of such a group, and half of those had plans to attend soon. These figures are inflated by the fact that many of the families were recruited from these groups. Such a high percentage would not be expected in other samples. Furthermore, the 88 percent of parents who did attend singles groups did not feel as strongly as those just quoted. Several had mixed feelings about the "hustling" atmosphere of PWP, and a few were adamantly opposed to PWP. "It's just like going to a bar; you feel like a piece of meat," said one woman. "It's very clique-ish. I went once and left very upset," reported a father. Nevertheless, fully half the parents counted PWP—or another singles group—among their most important sources of support.

Family

After singles groups, parents mentioned their own family of origin most frequently as members of their support network. Sixty-two percent of mothers and three-quarters of fathers reported that contact with their own parents or siblings had increased since the divorce. What exactly do these family members provide? As table 7-2 shows, they provide help in a variety of ways, from listening to problems to loaning money. Here are some representative comments regarding parents' feelings about relying on their own parents for help:

> My mother lives next door. I can confide in her about money problems, but not about men. She loans me money and signed for the telephone. She watches the kids a couple of hours a day. And the car is half hers. Without her, I couldn't go to work. (LPN, children are four and eight.)
> couldn't go to work. (LPN, children are four and eight.)

One of the fathers explained:

> My parents are retired and live ten miles away. My mother comes every morning and sees Maureen off to school. They do all my grocery shopping, which is a big help. They even took out a loan to help me pay the lawyers' fees to get custody of the kids. (Plumber, children are eight, thirteen, and fourteen.)

Only one father but one-quarter of the mothers resented the increased contact that had become necessary between their parents and themselves since the divorce. One father commented:

> I see my parents a couple of times a week now. That is twice as much as before. I'm close to my mother and value her support, but she intervenes too much. I have gone on dates and called home only to find that she had discovered they were alone and come over to sit with them. This makes me

Table 7-2
Percentage of Parents Whose Relatives Provide Supportive "Services"

| Custodian (n) | Type of Service | | | | |
	Confiding and Caring	Money	Regular Sitting	Car, Repairs	Laundry, Shopping
Mothers (16)	62%	37%	31%	31%	—
Fathers (16)	62	31	56	—	12
Joint mothers (16)	66	55	22	11	—
Joint fathers (16)	77	—	—	—	—

feel that I have to come home earlier, seeing as my mother is older. (Machinist, children are eleven, twelve, and fourteen.)

One mother lamented:

> I see my mother now for only one reason: because I use her car. I can't afford my own. I have the use of her car, but she wants me to jump and fetch things when she asks. She is no emotional support. If I told her about a problem, she would change the subject. She helps with money and buys clothes for the kids. We've learned to coexist, but we are hardly close. (Unemployed mother, daughters are thirteen and fourteen.)

Each of the mothers who resented the increased parental contact had increased it for the same reason as the mother just quoted—for help with money and other necessities. With the exceptions of the people just quoted, parents in the sample reported enjoying their increased contact with their parents and felt it was valued by their parents as it was by themselves.

Therapy

After singles groups and family, mothers relied on therapy more than fathers, and fathers relied more on dating than mothers. Both activities were important to parents in this sample. Sixty-nine percent of single mothers had sought some type of counseling—either before or after divorce, whereas only 38 percent of fathers and 19 percent of mothers were still seeing a therapist. Although fewer fathers sought therapy, those who did stayed longer. Fathers averaged 2.5 years, whereas mothers averaged 1.4 years. All parents were satisifed with the treatment they received. For example:

> The clinic saw Jimmy and me together. They are terrific. His behavior improved immensely; he started doing better in school. I calmed down and felt more in touch, and started to handle my kids better. (Unemployed mother, children are six and nine.)

One of the fathers said:

> I have been attending a therapy group for two years now. It meets five nights a week, and you can go as often as you want. There was a time right after the divorce when I had to go three times a week just to get enough emotional goodies to get through the next twenty-four hours. I needed a lot of attention and a place to cry. (Executive, daughter is seven.)

The only negative comments about counseling came from two mothers who had received nothing but medication from their therapists:

This psychiatrist was charging me $25 for ten minutes and giving me pills. I was groggy all the time and would sleep until 1 P.M. I could hardly think. I switched to a clinic for financial reasons. It costs me $1 to see a counselor there for a full hour, and I get so much help! She helps me get clear about my feelings and helps me solve problems with my son. (Avon representative, children are ten, fifteen, and sixteen.)

In comparison with the number of parents who entered therapy, very few of their children did. Only 19 percent of mothers and 19 percent of fathers had brought their children into treatment. These parents felt that the children had benefited a great deal from the experience, although some reported that their children had to be prodded to go. None of the parents whose children were not in therapy described themselves as "antitherapy." They simply did not feel the children needed treatment.

Dating

Fathers were more likely to be dating regularly than mothers. Table 7-3 shows that 94 percent of fathers were dating from twice a month to three times per week. Only 56 percent of mothers were dating this often—and nearly one-third had not dated at all since the divorce. The reasons for this had to do with not feeling "ready" to date. All denied that the presence of children affected their choice. Parents who *were* dating, however, did mention that the presence of children inhibited them in some ways. Half of the single-custody parents made such comments. Many felt that they had to "show a good example" to their children and so curtailed their sexual behavior:

I like my son to meet my dates. But on occasion while he was asleep, there has been a girl out here visiting. Things have gotten tacky, and then I go cold turkey thinking, "What if he woke up and found me in bed with a

Table 7-3
Percentage of Parents Who Date Regularly

| Dating Frequency | Custodian[a] (n) | | | |
	Mothers	Fathers	Joint Mothers	Joint Fathers[b]
Regularly	56%	94%	55%	77%
Periodically	13	6	22	—
Not at all	31	—	22	—

Note: *Regularly* is twice a month to three times a week.
[a]Fathers (single and joint) date more than mothers (single and joint). $X^2(1) = 10.42$; $p < .01$.
[b]The remaining 22 percent of joint fathers were already remarried or cohabiting with a woman.

woman?'' I could say, ''I was a married man; I have my needs.'' But he could say, ''I'm fourteen, and I have my needs too.'' I make some sacrifices for my son. (Salesman, son is thirteen.)

One of the mothers said:

I don't spend the night with a man as often as I'd like; I must set an example for them. (Paralegal, children are ten, fourteen, and sixteen.)

One father maintained that the children themselves had warned him not to date:

I've been busy and haven't had the chance to date. Also the kids have made it clear that they don't want me dating. The girls, who are not in my custody, are going through Oedipal stuff, I think. Merrill said, ''I'll kill you if you go with another woman.'' They say, ''You'll just get divorced again, Dad.'' (Lawyer, sons are twelve and fourteen.)

It is not clear to what extent some of the parents were actually projecting their own reticence about dating onto their children. A study of children's own views of their parents' dating would be most interesting.

Some of the mothers in the sample reported that their absention from dating had to do with anger toward men. Here is an example:

At first I hated men. My husband had me thinking I wasn't a person. And then with the divorce, it seemed that everyone you dealt with was a man. The lawyer was a man, the judge was a man—and their big thing was putting women down. (Therapy aid, children are ten and fifteen.)

Given these attitudes toward dating, it is not surprising that many more fathers than mothers were interested in remarriage.

Remarriage

Table 7-4 shows that whereas 56 percent of fathers definitely wished to remarry, only 25 percent of women did. Among the men desirous of remarriage, 22 percent were engaged to be married within weeks of the interview. When asked why they desired remarriage, parents mentioned their personal needs far more often than they mentioned the need for another parent for their children. Here is a typical comment:

I would hope to remarry. It would enhance my life. I'm not a loner. I'm a toucher and a feeler, and I like to share happiness and sadness. (Store manager, son is fourteen.)

Table 7-4
Percentage of Parents Who Desired to Remarry

| | Custodian[a] | | | |
	Mothers (16)	Fathers (16)	Joint Mothers[b] (9)	Joint Fathers[c] (9)
Definitely	25%	56%	33%	77%
Definitely not	44	19	22	—

[a]More fathers (single and joint) than mothers (single and joint) desired to remarry. $X^2(1) = 18.88$; $p < .001$.
[b]Includes 11 percent who were already married or engaged to marry within six months.
[c]Includes 33 percent who were already married or engaged to marry within six months.

Religion

A number of parents mentioned members of the clergy as part of their postdivorce support network. Parents were interviewed about how their religious faith had changed throughout the divorce process. Four mothers and fathers stated that they had become much more religious as a result of the divorce. Here is a representative comment:

> I don't know how I would have pulled through the divorce without my faith in God and the support of our church. Everything seemed to be shifting and changing in my life, but God was a constant. The minister in our church was incredibly kind. He would call to see what I was doing and even offered me some money when I was completely broke. (Teacher's aid, son is fifteen.)

Said a father:

> Prayer became extremely important to me at the time of the crisis, and it has stayed with me as a habit now that things have normalized again. (Salesman, son is thirteen.)

Twice as many parents, however, reported a major break from religion as a result of the divorce:

> The church had been a major source of identity in my life, and it went out of my life with the divorce. That was a crushing blow. When my husband left me with our seven children for another woman, I went straight to our pastor for guidance. The first advice I got was, "Apply for an annulment—you might want to remarry." They made me feel that I had done something wrong, and I had to get the church to forgive me. I went to see three priests—thinking I had just hit a sour one. I didn't want to remarry. I just wanted some emotional support. I wanted to know how to get through the night to see the next day. I was totally unsupported by the

church. It was my Protestant friends who helped me through it. The painful irony was that in addition to losing my long-time identity as a wife—and all that that meant—I also then had to deal with losing my religion as well. (High school teacher, children are eleven, fourteen, fifteen, and seventeen, at home).

One of the fathers spoke with sadness about the politics of attaining a church annulment:

Religion was important to me during the marriage. I went to the pastor to file a petition for a church divorce with the Chancellor of Cleveland. I filled out my half of the papers, but she wouldn't do hers. Then the pastor told me that even if she did, and even if I were granted a divorce, I couldn't remarry or keep company with other women—so I changed my mind. As time goes, I become more comfortable with not having religion. Talking to other Catholics, I've found that you can sometimes find a priest who will absolve you and even some who will remarry you in the church. It depends on the priest. The people who get them seem to be wealthy. (Machinist, children are eleven, twelve, and fourteen.)

A woman who still considered herself a member of the Catholic church said:

One priest told me I could receive the sacraments, and another told me, "You are still married to him." My friend said, "No wonder it's taking you so long to get over this. He's telling you you're still married to him." But the church has really gotten a lot better—a lot more open now. They even have started a support group for divorcees. (Avon representative, children are ten, fifteen, and sixteen.)

Several parents had a difficult time integrating their feelings about the divorce with what their children were being taught in catechism:

My kids go to religious instruction, and Mark came home and told me, "Divorce is a sin because at marriage you say, 'Till death do us part' and you are living in sin." I told Mark, "Living in sin" would be to go on the way we were before. (Student and secretary, children are seven, ten, and eleven.)

Social Stigma

Because this chapter is about the ways in which divorced parents cultivated social support, it seemed appropriate also to include issues concerning their problems in obtaining needed support. A section of the interview was devoted to *social stigma*, defined broadly to include any type of discrimination or perceived loss of respect in the community because of their status as divorced parents.

On the Rank-Stress scale, mothers ranked "social stigma" as more stressful than fathers—although both ranked the item fairly low. The interview data clearly explain this sex difference. It was hypothesized that men would have a more difficult time with social stigma because men who raise children are departing from their traditional gender role. The opposite proved true, however; single mothers had far greater problems with social stigma.

Table 7-5 shows that 94 percent of single mothers had suffered some type of discrimination because of their divorced status. Only one-third of fathers had experienced discrimination. Over half of the men, moreover, felt that being a single parent actually *enhanced* their social status.

The Mothers

Among the mothers who had experienced discrimination, over half had had trouble obtaining credit; one-third had trouble finding an apartment, and 20 percent had had problems with the neighborhood and jobs. The credit and apartment problems were recounted in chapter 3 because they related directly to economics. Here are examples of other types of exclusion:

> The children have been discriminated against in the neighborhood. Other kids are not allowed to spend the night at our house. They are allowed to go to the other kids' houses, however, where they will be "properly supervised." (High school teacher, children are eleven, fourteen, fifteen, and seventeen.)

Said another mother:

> I have learned to lie to employers. I told one I have an aunt down the street, because they asked me what I would do about taking care of the children

Table 7-5
Percentage of Parents Who Felt that Single Parenthood Enhanced or Diminished Their Social Status

| | Custodian (n) | | | |
Change in Status	Mothers (16)	Fathers (16)	Joint Mothers (9)	Joint Fathers (9)
Diminished	94%	31%	77%	33%
Enhanced	—	56	—	22
No change	6	13	22	44

Note: More mothers (single and joint) than fathers (single and joint) felt their status was diminished. $X^2(1) = 74$; $p < .0001$.

while I worked. Sure it's illegal for them to ask those questions, and men are never asked such things at interviews. But if I want a job, it makes more sense for me to lie than to get a lawsuit. (Student and secretary, children are seven, ten, and eleven.)

Several mothers expressed the belief that women in general are treated with less respect in society and that being divorced means that a woman is more often in situations without a man. Thus after divorce, women face additional disrespect:

Any time a woman approaches a business, you have to be careful. They assume a woman is stupid and will try to take advantage of you. At the school they listen with one ear. My husband used to call them about things, and he commanded respect from them. When the kids' dog died and they were so upset I called their guidance counselor to mention it—and they acted like I was nuts. (Student and secretary, children are seven, ten, and eleven.)

Said another mother:

In marriage my husband would have gone to the garage to fix the car. Now I have to go—and they're snotty and disrespectful—the TV repairman too, and the teachers. They treat you like you're stupid and will laugh in your face. (Avon representative, children are ten, fifteen, and sixteen.)

The Fathers

The situation for fathers looked considerably different. Over half the fathers made comments of this nature:

I'm treated with a lot more respect than when I was married. Most people think a guy who can raise two kids—especially babies—is all right. There's a guy at work I don't get along with. He's hotheaded and prejudiced, and yet he came up and told me he had a lot of respect for me. (Toolmaker, children are eight and nine.)

Said another father:

I feel that being a single father has been a plus when it comes to feeling respected by people. I was afraid that women wouldn't want to go out with me because I had custody of my daughter, but the reverse has been true. They feel, I guess, that here is a caring and sensitive man. (Executive, daughter is seven.)

This man's account seems particularly ironic in contrast with the problems the women had:

> Being a single father helped me get this apartment. I wanted one in this building, but it doesn't take children. But the landlord is also a single father, so he said, "I'll take care of it." (Salesman, son is thirteen.)

One father took an ironic view of the fuss people made over him:

> People act like I'm a hero and ask "How can you do it?" [work and raise a child] How does anybody do it? Women have been doing it for years. (Professor, son is seven.)

There were, however, five fathers who gave examples of being treated unfairly because of their status:

> The company called me in and asked if anything about my job had led to the divorce. They told me I could be passed up for promotion because of the divorce. It's a family-oriented company. They feel if you can't handle problems at home, how can you handle company problems? But I did get all my raises, so I don't know what that was all about. (Salesman, son is thirteen.)

Said another father:

> I wonder about one incident. I was up for promotion, and usually, anyone nominated gets it and I didn't. They check over your background like the FBI. I don't know if it was the divorce, but I suspect so because it meant a transfer to a really conservative community. That made me angry, but I couldn't prove anything. (Security guard, children are thirteen and fourteen.)

The father with the most problems in this area had been divorced ten years prior to the interview, when custodial fathers were even fewer than they are now:

> In 1974, four years after the divorce, the children were awarded to me by the judge. I had even entered them in school the previous fall. The teacher said she had no obligation to talk to me or give me information. I called the principal who said the same thing. I called a lawyer and the school superintendent. The latter made them back down. I think a lot of fathers get the brush-off because they're not assertive. In scouts they don't want fathers around because scouts are run by women. They are married women who are threatened by divorced men. I haven't had any of these problems for several years now. Things are beginning to change. (Psychiatrist, children are fifteen and seventeen.)

Children's Support Systems

It is not surprising that the support networks of the children in the sample also changed in significant ways. The first question that comes to mind is whether or not the noncustodial parent was still a member of the child's support group.

The majority of parents in the sample (twenty out of thirty-two) reported that the noncustodial parent was less involved with the children prior to the divorce—to the point of having no meaningful relationship with them. An additional quarter of the mothers and fathers said that the visiting parent was less involved than before but still maintained a meaningful relationship with them. One father and two mothers reported that their ex-spouses were *more* involved with the children than before. These exceptions are of particular interest:

> My ex-husband is actually more involved with the kids now than when we were married. When he takes time to talk with them now, he really talks. When they were little, they were just there; he ignored them. They were my responsibility. The fact that he doesn't know what subjects they have or what teachers is irrelevant. He didn't know before either. But now he relates to them as people. (Paralegal, children are ten, fourteen, and sixteen.)

Said another mother:

> He is more involved with Jerry now. He doesn't take Jerry for granted. Yes, I would say they have a very significant relationship. They are close—they do sports together, and they talk, and you can tell they miss each other if one should get sick and not make it on Sunday. (Nurse, son is nine.)

The fact that so many parents felt the visiting parent was no longer a significant other led to the next question: Did parents feel it was necessary to replace the nonresident parent with other caring adults? All the custodial mothers and fathers—except those whose ex-spouses were still involved with the children—said yes. Opinion was divided as to whether or not it was important to find the child another adult of the absent parent's sex:

> When he is having a temper blast, he needs a man. He needs to see how a man handles this kind of situation. I don't solve problems that way. I'm a woman. So far I haven't been able to find somebody for him. The Big Brother program told me they have to respond first to kids with problems. (Store manager, son is fifteen.)

Said another mother:

> I think both boys and girls need a male model in order to develop normally. I worried out loud to my counselor that my son would become gay and my girls would go after every man they saw, and he laughed. I decided not to worry too much about it, but I watch. . . . (Student and secretary, children are seven, ten, and eleven.)

Some of the fathers had similar ideas about the importance of a person in their children's lives who is of the same sex as the noncustodian:

> Marty and I are very close, but there are things he can't get from me that he could get from a woman. When he's hurt, I can't console him in the same way as a woman can. I'm sorry—I just don't think a man can do it. When Marty was sick last winter, his mother came over with home-made soup, and she pampered him for a whole day, and he just perked up amazingly. (Salesman, son is thirteen.)

Said another father, obviously distressed:

> Linda is thirteen, and she's gonna become a young lady soon, and I worry about it every day because I'm not the one to tell her about it. The women at PWP have come up to me and offered, and my mother is always there. I have to talk to them about it soon, or I'll be sorry. (Mechanic, daughters are four, eight, twelve, and thirteen.)

There were as many parents, however, who believed that while a support group for the children was important, the sex of the adults in question was not paramount. Here are some representative comments:

> Kids, I think, don't so much need a person around of the opposite sex as they need a number of interesting and loving people in their lives. One person is absolutely, positively not enough for kids. I think that intense exposure to one person is crippling. (LPN, children are four and eight.)

Said one father:

> Well, sure children need a role model of their own sex—but those models are everywhere. They've had women teachers since kindergarten. And they have aunts and grandmothers and cousins who are female. I have never at any point felt the need to find a surrogate mother for them, although I am always conscious of wanting them to have a number of adults they can count on for advice and hugs and kisses. (High school principal, children are twelve and fourteen.)

Nearly all the parents in the sample had been successful in their efforts to enhance the support circle for their children. The adults who joined these circles were teachers, relatives, lovers, neighbors, "Big Brothers," and one therapist. Here are the parents' comments:

> I was concerned for Ben because he had two sisters and me, and a female exchange student who lived with us, and no father. It was then that Elliot came into our lives—and he became everyone's big brother. He was close to us for years—the whole time he was in college. And after he graduated, he still wrote and called, and just recently the kids went to visit him in

New York where he now lives. . . . We've had some wonderful people in our lives since the divorce. My brother-in-law became close with the kids. And they have really loved some of my men friends. And, of course, there are friends they don't like, and they pick out their faults with an unerring eye! (Paralegal, children are ten, fourteen, and sixteen.)

Said another mother:

They have become very close to my sister, Sylvie. She lives nearby, and they float over there every day, and her kids know they can do the same. My son also admires his football coach a lot. And they both spend a lot of time playing with my boyfriend. He has more energy than I do, and I think he spends more time playing with them than I do. (LPN, children are four and eight.)

The custodial fathers' comments touched the same themes:

There is no doubt in my mind that my daughter has more love in her life than ever. We have become close to my aunt and uncle who are really crazy about Jeannette, and they hug and kiss her in a way her own mother never did. We also do things with the woman I date and her two girls. (Executive, daughter is seven.)

One father remarked:

I have more friends and more support than when I was married, and all of my friends are in some way in contact also with my children. I mentioned before how important PWP is to me. Well, it's important to the kids too; they go to all the kids' functions. There are picnics and hikes, and the older ones have discussion groups. I thought it would be good for them to be with older kids who were in the same situation they were in. They'll nag me sometimes if I don't want to go. (Machinist, children are eleven, twelve, and fourteen.)

Most of the children, the older ones particularly, named adults with whom they had become close after the divorce. Nearly all the children denied any suggestion that such adults served as a substitute for their nonresident parent. They preferred to think of these individuals as friends. Here are some of their comments:

Well, I became really close to my mom's brother who lived with us for several years after my dad left. He was really nice to us, and he would take me out and play football, and play golf because he loved golf. It was like having an older brother around because he's much younger than my mom. I could even go to him sometimes when I didn't want to tell my mother. And we're still close even though he moved out four years ago. (Seventeen-year-old girl in mother's custody.)

A fourteen-year-old boy said:

> Well, I became very good friends with my flute teacher. She is this in-
> credibly good musician and outasite teacher, and we would always talk
> about stuff after my lesson. She was the only one I told that my parents
> were splitting up. And I was so messed up about it that my mother wanted
> me—you know—to see a shrink. And I kinda wanted to, but I thought,
> "Who—me? Am I crazy?" and so I told Dana, my teacher, about it, and
> you know what? She told me she goes to a shrink too—twice a week!
> (Fourteen-year-old boy in mother's custody.)

An eight-year-old girl had become attached to her father's girl friend,
whom her father was to marry within weeks of the interview:

> Yes, I did get close to some people. I got close to Margie. Margie is really
> nice, and she always fixes my hair and reads to me and teaches me how to
> cook mashed potatoes. . . . My mommy didn't play with us too much
> because she used to drink. (Eight-year-old girl, in father's custody.)

There were a few questions in the interview about changes in sibling relationships after divorce. My impression from the responses of both parents
and children is that younger children tended to fight more after the divorce
and older siblings tended to get along better with each other after the
divorce. One possible interpretation of this situation is that *all* children
want more closeness with their siblings after divorce and that younger
children achieve increased contact by fighting whereas older children
achieve it through confiding in each other. Further exploration of sibling
issues was beyond the scope of this study. Some fascinating work in this
area is now being done by Mary Reeves at the Philadelphia Child Guidance
Clinic.

There was one maternal-custody family in the study whose support
system was palpably rich and deep. The interview with this family happened
to take place just days after they had moved into a new house, and unpacking and repairs were in progress as we talked. On entering the home, I was
introduced to two friends of the mother's who were painting. A man whom
the mother was currently dating was fixing the washing machine. Two of
the children were unpacking books, and the fourteen-year-old boy was
upstairs doing homework with a classmate. I was introduced to each of
these people either by the mother or by one of the children who seemed very
comfortable with all their guests. After the interview we all gathered for tea
and admired the repaired washing machine. Many people over the years, I
learned, had entered their lives—Elliot, their Big Brother, an aunt whose
children filtered back and forth between houses, and a teacher who became
attached to the sixteen-year-old girl. They seemed to represent a kind of
ideal postdivorce family. Their warmth and resourcefulness made them all

very attractive people. The mother was very proud of their lifestyle, but she was not uncritical of it. Her final statement about the issue of support systems deserves quoting:

> There is no doubt that my children would not have had so many interesting people in their lives if not for the divorce. But that can't compare with having a father! There is no doubt that I'm a happier person, and I tend to *think* that they are too, but I can't *know* if that will turn out to be the case. The data are not all in. (Paralegal, children are ten, fourteen, and sixteen.)

Joint Custody

Loneliness

Like the single parents, loneliness was ranked very high by joint parents. Joint fathers ranked it as their number 1 stressor, and mothers ranked it number 2. One difference in the reasons for loneliness described by joint- and single-custody parents was that many of the latter felt that the full burden of child rearing was a source of loneliness that loomed large. None of the joint parents cited that as a cause of loneliness. Instead, their accounts centered around the absence of an intimate relationship. Here is one example:

> At first it was terrible. The person who knew me best was saying she didn't love me, and that meant I was completely unlovable. With time and new relationships, of course, that has improved a lot. (Joint father G, musician, daughter is eight, alternate years.)

Support Groups

What do joint parents do to cope with loneliness? As in the case of single-custody parents, their support groups had changed a great deal since the divorce. Table 7-1 showed that 66 percent of joint mothers and 66 percent of joint fathers felt that there was almost no overlap between their pre- and postdivorce support groups. Their comments were similar to those of the single parents, that is, that some friends had drifted away from them, and that as a single, one wants to socialize with other singles.

Beyond the replacement of married friends with singles, the postdivorce support networks are larger than the predivorce networks. Again, nearly one-third of the joint parents said that their spouse had been their support "group" during the marriage. As was the case with single-custody parents, the postdivorce support groups included therapists, singles groups, extended family, and dates.

Singles Groups. Fewer joint parents than single-custody parents mentioned singles groups as important features of their postdivorce lives. Nearly half the joint parents, however, *did* belong to some other kind of group that they had joined after the divorce for emotional help. These groups welcomed divorced parents, but were not designed solely for them. They included: men's groups, women's groups, an "extended family" organized through the Unitarian Church, and a lesbian organization. (This difference may simply reflect the recruitment process; fewer joint families were recruited from singles groups than were the other families.) Here are some representative comments on the usefulness of these groups:

> I go to the Alternative at the Unitarian Church. They have activities where you go into one of two groups. One group does a psychological game, and the other does a musical exercise. Then the groups get back together for refreshments and you have something to talk about. (Joint mother X, social worker, children are six, seven, nine, ten, and twelve, split week.)

Said one father:

> I joined an extended family through the church. It's people of all ages and professions who believe in the idea of an extended family. We go to picnics together and sports events. The kids love it. We've met some real nice people through that. It's important because we don't have any relatives of our own in Buffalo. (Joint father F, CPA, children are five and nine, split year.)

The father who had started a men's group said:

> Several of us who were in transition of one type or another saw the women we knew bonding together in women's groups and feeling really strong and close as a result. We realized that we too needed to examine the ways our socialization has limited our potential as people. It was this group of men that got me through the divorce. It was there that I could cry and feel safe and supported. The group continued to meet for years. (Joint father D, professor, children are twelve and fourteen, split week.)

Family. The next most often cited support was the family. Over half the joint mothers and half the joint fathers reported that contact with either their parents or siblings had increased because of the divorce. Table 7-2 showed that joint mothers, like single mothers, rely on their relatives for a variety of favors. Joint fathers, on the other hand, relied on their relatives only for confiding and caring. Note that whereas 55 percent of joint mothers received financial help from the family, none of the joint fathers did. How did mothers feel about this financial help? Half were uneasy about it and mentioned the importance of paying back family loans as soon as possible so as not to be dependent on parents. Said one joint mother:

> Yes, it bothers me very much to take money from my parents. Why? Because thirty-six is a little old to be supported by your mother. The other

reason I don't like it is that it puts more pressure on me to be aggressive with
my ex to fight for support. I can't explain to them I'm just tired. I've been
fighting a long time. (Joint mother A, doctoral student, children are six and
twelve, split week.)

In addition to relatives, best friends and colleagues at work were also mentioned as important. Said one father evocatively:

People were so great—inviting me over a lot so I wouldn't be alone. Just
stopping in the hall to ask how I was doing. I had the image of por-
poises—how when one porpoise is injured, the others gather together and
bring him to the surface so he can breathe again. (Joint father H, musician,
daughter is eight, alternating years.)

The biggest difference between the joint- and single-custody parents on this
question of family help is that joint parents did not rely on their parents for
regular babysitting. This is undoubtedly due to the fact that joint parents rely
on each other for child care.

Therapy. Seventy-seven percent of the joint mothers had been in therapy
either before, during, or after divorce, whereas only 44 percent of joint
fathers had. Again, men stayed in therapy an average of 1.8 years, whereas
mothers remained an average of 1.17 years. One joint mother said she had
decided on a therapeutic alternative to the couch:

Instead of putting all that money toward a psychiatrist, I decided to spend
it on flying lessons—which provides me with a feeling of relaxation, confidence, and pampering myself a bit. It's something I've always wanted to
do, and I love it.

Only one-third of the families had brought their children into treatment.
One father described the children's need for counseling in an especially sensitive way:

I think therapy is important because a kid needs to vent just like an adult
does. And the kid's parent is not always the best person because sometimes
what you need to vent is lies and little half-truths. My relationship with my
kids is twenty times better since they've seen a counselor. (Joint father Z, in-
surance salesman, children are five, nine, and twelve, split week.)

Dating. Twenty-two percent of joint parents had not dated since the
divorce. As was the case with single-custody parents, joint fathers dated
more than joint mothers. One joint father was married at the time of the interview; two were married within months of the interview, and one was living
with a woman. All the others dated weekly or more.

Parents were asked about their problems in dating. Many spoke of adjusting their dating to their children's needs:

> I don't have men come to the house on nights when the kids are here. My older son gets annoyed at being blocked out of the living room. He reacts to women, too, who take up too much of my time. No, it's not a big sacrifice to date on the other nights. (Joint mother A, doctoral student, children are six and twelve, split week.)

Said a joint father:

> My sexual behavior is inhibited. I wouldn't want them to know I was sleeping with a woman. It might confuse them. They might think the relationship was more serious than it was. (Joint father F, architect, children are five and nine, split year.)

But some parents felt no hindrance at all because of children:

> I have no problems with the girls' meeting my dates. Or even spending the night. The kids are very comfortable and open kids. (Joint mother C, real-estate agent, daughters are nine and ten, split day.)

One father mentioned that it bothered his dates more than his children:

> The kids don't inhibit me as much as they inhibit the people I date. In one relationship it was a major problem. But I am becoming less tolerant of friends who see my children as obstacles, so that it deprives me of what I need. I will not let a friend use the children as an excuse for withholding sex, for example. (Joint father E, professor, children are ten, fifteen, and sixteen, split week.)

The lesbian mother described her situation in this way:

> Both kids know I'm gay. Matt definitely had a hostile reaction for a while. When he was ten years old, his baby sister was born, and then the divorce, and then he finds out his mother is gay. He was afraid I didn't value him as a male. He felt rejected, and it was hard for him to express except through being obstinate. We had terrible fights. But it's been a few years now, and things have normalized. He and I are very close now. And he likes Andrea. We have all gone on vacation together. (Joint mother E, student, children are four and fourteen, split week.)

The comments of this mother's son on her sexual preference were candid and informative:

> Well, I had never had a prejudice or nothing against gay people. But then when you find out your own mother is gay—wow! That was a real shocker!

At first it seemed so weird. And then I was mad because I thought it meant she only liked women and didn't like men at all. I mean I *knew* that wasn't true, but I just used to think about it. Then my friends would say things to make fun of some kid and call him a faggot or something, and I would think, Jesus! If they only knew! But it's no big deal, really. I don't go around telling my friends my Ma is gay because it's none of their business. . . . My mother is still the same. We fight all the time, and it has nothing to do with Andrea. (Boy, fourteen, split week.)

Remarriage. One-third of the joint fathers are remarried as of this writing. An additional 44 percent said they would definitely like to remarry, and the remainder said it was a possibility. Only one joint mother is remarried as of this writing, and only 22 percent definitely want to remarry. Again, the greater emotional neediness of the men (as indicated by their ranking loneliness, their number one problem) is reflected in their tendency to remarry.

Stigma. Seventy-seven percent of the joint mothers but only one-third of the fathers cited at least one instance of discrimination due to their divorced status. Here is one mother's account of a life riddled with small prejudices:

I am treated differently by my family because they think I've gone astray. And if one of my kids is having a problem, my friends will say that it's obviously because of the "home situation. . . ." Also, in the hardware store they'll tell you, "Ask your husband." I have said, "I don't have anyone to ask," and then they're on the make. . . . Jimmy, it turned out, is hypoglycemic, like me, but the teacher refused to believe it because she assumed his behavior problem was due to the divorce. (Joint mother Z, student and waitress, children are five, nine, and twelve, split week.)

Said another mother:

We have always had joint custody but recently switched to having them based with their father. This meant I had to look for apartments telling them I lived alone but that my children, who were based with their father, spent part of each week with me. I went through six months of struggle just over, "What will people think of me when I tell them that?" And I had heard that they don't like to rent to single women anyway because they don't want men spending the night. (Joint mother G, occupational therapist, children are eleven and fifteen, unstructured.)

One-third of the fathers recounted problems of diminished social status caused by the divorce:

There are sitters who can't sit for me. I don't know this for a fact, but there were sitters who used to love to babysit but who are no longer available. I suspect they have been forbidden to sit for me because I'm a single man.

I also don't get invited out to dinner as much because they don't want an odd person at the table. (Joint father B, college administrator, children are five and nine, split week.)

Said another father:

Women feel sorry for me and want to mother me, or they want no part of me because I have kids. Even at the level of dating they're turned off. Some hesitate because they're looking for a long-term relationship. Some assume I want a wife, but I have no intentions of remarrying. So everyone has their own prejudice. Dating is not the simple matter it was as a single man. (Joint father F, architect, children are five and nine, split year.)

Another man lamented:

As a single man, women assume you're an animal. It is a problem because women are on guard a lot. And I'm sure they should be because I know a lot of men, and a lot are really pigs. It's a problem for me because I'm shy to begin with. (Joint father E, lawyer, children are four and fourteen, split week.)

Despite these negative experiences, two of the joint fathers felt that their social status was enhanced by the divorce:

When people find out I'm raising kids, they are very complimentary. There is sympathy for fathers. (Joint father C, CPA, children are nine and ten, split day.)

Another said:

Being divorced is a positive thing in terms of invitations. I'm a better person to invite to cocktail parties because I'm single. (Joint father G, professor, children are eleven and fifteen, unstructured.)

Conclusions

I hypothesized that men would have greater familiarity with problems of social stigma than women because their parenting defines them outside their gender role. The expectation was that fathers would be less welcome at school functions and would have a harder time feeling accepted in their neighborhood and finding dates than would single women. The opposite proved true. Men felt divorced parenthood elevated their status, and women felt that it lowered theirs.

It was striking that although the fathers experienced less social stigma than mothers and dated more than mothers, they nevertheless experienced more loneliness than mothers. This finding appears even more dramatic considering that the men in this study were atypical in that they all had custody of their children (either sole or joint). Most men after divorce are left with no family at all. Bloom (1978) cites this loss of family as a reason that separated and divorced men enter psychiatric care at rates at least six times those of married men.

My impression, based on these interviews, is that while men are capable of constructing a support group among whom there is caring and mutual aid, they find it difficult to create adult-adult relationships in which there is genuine intimacy. One fourth of the fathers, in fact, stated that there was *no one, either before or after the divorce,* in whom they confided. They did not present this as a loss, but as a fact about their personality. They were "independent." One man explained repeatedly that he was a "Leo," which meant that he did not need any emotional support.

This difference between men and women can be partly explained in terms of early sex-role socialization. Women, more than men, are trained to be self-disclosing and relationship oriented. This also elucidates the fact that men dated more than women, while women entered therapy more often than men. Girls are trained to express feelings and seek help, whereas boys are trained to be socially aggressive, for example, to propose dates rather than wait to be asked.

The fact that all parents, and especially fathers, were still lonely at the time of the interview, does not mean that these individuals were not coping successfully. Loneliness is pandemic in postindustrial societies. On the contrary, the support networks of these informants seem in many cases to be better developed than those of their married life. Recall that many adults said that their ex-spouse had been their support group, whereas they could now rely on a variety of people. A more complex support group is potentially more exciting, more colorful, and safer as well, for if one aspect fails, many remain.

The parents did not give the impression that they would have preferred the support of one person to the multifaceted system they had after divorce, although many *also* longed for a new partner. It would seem that as in any question of breadth and depth, the best of all worlds is to have both breadth and depth. When that is impossible, one may substitute for the other, although they are not interchangeable.

In this light, it is no wonder that one woman's fantasy for a living arrangement (while she was unsuccessfully seeking a landlord who would rent to her) was:

> a dream of buying a big house with private bedrooms, where a number of single parents and their children would live, to share the cooking and the caring.

Notes

1. Now a classic is Robert Weiss's *Marital Separation* (New York: Basic Books, 1975). See also Weiss's *Going it alone* (New York: Basic Books, 1979).

2. J. Bowlby, *Attachment and loss,* vol. 1: *Attachment* (New York: Basic Books, 1969).

8   Conclusions

The purpose of this study was to compare the family realities created by maternal, paternal, and joint custody. As expected, the dissolution of the marital dyad changed the way the family performed each of its tasks. In general, the restructuring of the family after divorce required the following processes:

1. The parents adopted cross-gender skills. The mothers became more involved in the world of work and began driving, managing money, maintaining a car, and so on. The fathers began investing less of themselves in their work. Many shortended their hours in order to spend more time with their children. They learned to cook, sew, and do laundry.

2. The children's roles in the family also changed. Even the younger children were given more responsibilities around the house—as well as more decision-making power within the family.

3. The family's relationship with the outside world changed in a way that expanded its boundaries to include more of the community. Whereas the predivorce home had been self-contained, the postdivorce support network included neighbors, dates, church friends, Big Brothers, therapists, and PWP confreres.

There were exceptions to these generalizations, but in the majority of families, these changes did take place.

Children's Adjustment in the Three Custody Types

No evidence emerged from this study that would support a legal presumption for maternal custody. On all measures of children's psychological adjustment, there were no differences by custody type. The emotional climate, as measured during the story-telling task, was as positive in families headed by a father as in those headed by a mother.

The only variable that predicted poorer adjustment in children was parental conflict. Children whose parents remained embattled after the divorce were more likely to score low on the Piers-Harris Self-Concept Scale. These children tended also to be rated by their parents as having more behavior problems.

Although the amount of visitation with the noncustodian did *not* statistically predict poor adjustment, most single-custody children were dissatisfied with the amount of visitation they had. This was not the case with joint-custody children, however, most of whom were content with their arrangement.

More important than the quantity of time spent with each parent was the quality of time. It was clear that the children in joint custody had retained a filial relationship with both parents. The single-custody children, in contrast, seemed to have an avuncular relationship with their noncustodian.

An important concern about joint custody discussed in the introduction was that it might promote parental conflict—or at least allow it to endure. This was not the case for the families in this study. Joint-custody parents did not report more conflict than the single-custody parents. In fact, whereas half of the latter had returned to court to fight about money, none of the joint parents had.

Each type of custody has its particular advantages and disadvantages. Some of these are listed in figure 8-1. Figure 8-1 reflects one of the central conclusions of the study, that is, that among the families investigated, joint custody had more advantages and fewer disadvantages than either maternal or paternal custody. This conclusion invariably leads to the question, "Is joint custody then for everyone?"

Joint Custody: The Answer?

The mental-health community appears to be divided into two camps on the question of joint custody. In one camp are clinicians who believe that joint custody is just an excuse for parents to stay married and to triangulate children into their love-hate dance. In the other camp are clinicians who believe that joint custody would cure a host of divorce-related ills such as defaults in child support and parental child snatching. Some even contend that if parents knew they would be bound to retain responsibility for their children, they would take more seriously the decision to have children in the first place.

Much more research is needed before we could conclude with confidence what the best custodial arrangements for children of different ages would be. Research on how joint custody works under conditions of varying parental enthusiasm will be extremely helpful. The new California law will result in many more awards of joint custody. California thus provides us with a laboratory where our hypotheses about children's best interests can be tested.

My conclusion, based on these fifty families, is that joint custody at its best is superior to single-parent custody at *its* best. My prediction is that

	Custody Type	
Major Problem	*Mothers (Single and Joint)*	*Fathers (Single and Joint)*

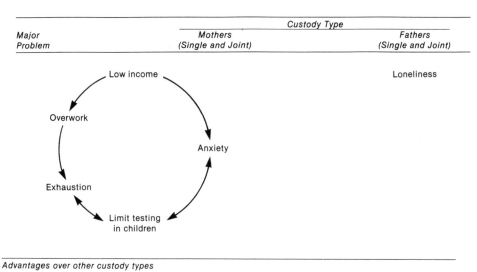

Loneliness

Advantages over other custody types			
Mothers	*Fathers*	*Joint Mothers*	*Joint Fathers*
1. Fewer custody fights than with paternal or joint custody	1. Less discrimination in housing and credit	1. Fewer court battles over money than single-parent custody	
2. Free to take children and leave town	2. Free to take children and leave town	2. More likely than single mothers to receive support from ex	2. Less discrimination in housing and credit
		3. Built-in break from parenting	
		4. Have perspective of two parents in disciplining	
		5. Can rely on each other for child care	

Disadvantages in relation to other custody types			
Mothers	*Fathers*	*Joint Mothers*	*Joint Fathers*
1. Overwhelmed by 100 percent responsibility for children; no break from parenting		1. Tied to ex-spouse, e.g., cannot leave town	
2. Less likely to receive support from ex than joint mothers	2. Need more substitute care than joint parents	2. Hassles of shuttling kids between two houses	
3. Need more substitute care than joint parents but can barely afford it	3. Miss the perspective of another adult in disciplining, etc.		
4. Miss the perspective of a second adult in disciplining, etc.			

Figure 8-1. Pros and Cons for Parents of Each Custody Type

more families will elect joint custody in the near future. Recall that many of the single-custody parents in this study had not heard of joint custody. When more families begin coparenting, there will be more available examples of how it is done. Its social acceptability will probably rise correspondingly.

One important finding from the joint families in this study is that they had had to change their arrangements over the years to suit their changing conditions. Many had relied on a trusted friend or relative to facilitate their negotiations over the years. Not all couples are fortunate enough to have such a person, and many must rely on the courts to make changes in their agreements. A new service, called "divorce mediation," is gaining in popularity. Mediators, who are sometimes employed by the court and sometimes employed privately, attempt to help couples negotiate the details of custody agreements. The growth of such services may make joint custody a viable alternative for more families.

Many Kinds of Families

More controversial than these conclusions about custody, perhaps, is the finding that the sample as a whole was not psychologically impaired. Recall that only eight children out of ninety-one scored a low self-concept according to standardized norms. Only two children out of those eight had a record of serious acting out. All eight children had a history of problems that predated the divorce. Only a handful of children in the sample had ever been brought for treatment.

It is crucial to remember that these families were studied for only four to six hours. My presuppositions, moreover, may have led to an underestimation of pathology. These factors notwithstanding, the contrast between this sample and others reported in the literature is striking. Wallerstein and Kelly, for example, wrote that they did not find a "victimless divorce." Those authors described children—even five years after divorce—as seriously depressed, and they reported "delinquent behavior, including arson, drug involvement, stealing, breaking and entering, and school failure" among the adolescents.[1]

Due to sampling problems in both studies, it simply is not possible to know if the "average" divorcing family looks more like my families or more like Wallerstein's and Kelly's. It is possible, however, to explain theoretically how such disparate outcomes are possible.

Such a theoretical task must begin with an analysis of the intact family, which is the source of all divorced families. Insight into this set of issues is provided by Christopher Lasch in *The Culture of Narcissism.* Lasch contends that the American family of the modern period, although patriarchal, is essentially *father absent*. That is, even when two married parents live together, the father is more often than not a "tired night visitor." This observation is supported by a recent study that showed the average father spends only twleve minutes per day interacting with his children.[2] Due to the alienating quality of much modern labor, the husband often returns home emotionally unavailable to his wife. The result of this father absence is that the mother—particularly the unemployed mother—seeks in her children the emotional fulfillment she does not receive from her husband. In structural language,[3] one could say that the average family contains a peripheral father and an overinvolved mother. The stresses on each family member due to this arrangement are patent. Men become increasingly isolated in the family and invest more of themselves in their work. They spend their days with other repressed adults and lose the spontaneity and sensuality that come from being with children. Women feel a sense of loss at the absence of contact with other adults. They may hear their vocabulary eroding from speaking only with individuals under age ten. In some families the mother begins to rely on an older child as her confidant—who may become almost a surrogate spouse. In other families, a mother's overinvolvement leads to infantilizing of a child. In either case, the individual identity of the children is sacrificed. The children in these "intact" families never really know their fathers, who are nominally "the boss," but who appear too removed to have real authority. Symptoms often develop as a result of these "normal" family boundaries.

The family structure just described is no historical accident, according to critical theory. It is, most fundamentally, the product of industrialization, which first removed the father from the home. This family structure, however, has served the needs of *advanced* capitalism as well. For example, the isolation of the nuclear family clearly serves to stimulate consumption. In the average suburb, instead of sharing resources, each family must have its *own* laundry machines, lawn mower, snow plow and swimming pool.

It is precisely because of the nuclear family's isolation that a family can indeed fall apart when divorce occurs. It can also regroup, however, and proceed with new strength. Let us consider further these two possibilities. The first scenario, with which clinicians have become familiar, is as follows: At the time of the separation, one parent—usually the father—leaves the home. The mother is left in dire financial straits and is more emotionally needy than before. She seeks in her children even more emotional sustenance. The family thus becomes more isolated, and the mother-child bond, more enmeshed.

In the other scenario, the custodial parent is convinced from the outset that the children cannot be raised by one person alone. Instead of closing ranks, this parent opens the boundaries of the family. In the best of situations, this includes maintaining the other parent fully involved with the children. Both parents reach outside the household for love and support. Thus mother and child can become more autonomous, and father and child can become closer than they were in the "intact" home.

Most of the joint-custody parents and many of the single-custody parents in this study clearly had enacted for themselves the second scenario. Approximately half of the mothers had gone out to work for the first time and described their new self-confidence and exhilaration that came from being out of the house—driving on freeways, making money, and having daily contact with other adults. Whereas the husband had been their support system, the support network of the postdivorce family included a much larger slice of the community.

The point of this analysis is not to extol divorce. There is no doubt that divorce is a painful process. It can be debilitating for children and adults—producing long-term suffering. It can also be corrective, however, leading to higher levels of functioning. To see divorce not as the disease but as the symptom is a critical change of focus. It may not influence at all what a given lawyer or therapist does to help a given family, but it is nonetheless critical. At this moment in history there are cries of "Save the family!" coming from all political sides. The "new right" is very disturbed about the high divorce rate. Their solution is a romatic return to the family of the 1950s. Their "Family Protection Act" proposes to save the family by returning prayer to schools, prohibiting the redefinition of sex roles, and exempting homosexuals from protection by the Civil Rights Act.[4]

The left too is distressed at the divorce rate, and there is a strong desire on the left to improve the viability of family life. The question is whether or not the nuclear family is the type of family to try to fortify. This analysis has attempted to show that *the problems that divorced families face are the very same problems—in kind if not in magnitude—that plague the "intact" family,* that is, absent father, overinvolved mother, and isolation from the community. The position of critical theory is that the family form worth "saving" is one that does not take these weaknesses for granted. The family form that might support a just social order would be one in which both parents take responsibility for child care, and both feel free to work outside the home. It would be a family in which children and adults could count on the support of people and institutions outside the family.

A "protection act" for this type of family would push for adequate child-care facilities, paid work leaves for fathers as well as mothers, job schedules with flex-time, and daycare facilities in offices and factories. Sweden has introduced a host of these changes in the past decade.[5] There have been hints of changes in the organization of American labor, but rampant conservatism may halt such experimentation.

As services shrink, communities may begin to organize themselves informally. (Such organization, ironically, could be the best of possible outcomes.) What exactly will happen as the demand for resources increases while supply dwindles is one of several areas meriting serious research attention.

Future Investigation

This study points to a number of urgent research questions. The first has already been mentioned—that is, the issue of how joint custody works for children of all ages under varying conditions of parental enthusiasm. Replication of studies such as this one with larger samples will help fill in the data gap. Such studies should also include families where the parents have *remarried*. The presence of new partners can change the character of the postdivorce family for better or worse and usually both. For the sake of simplicity, remarried parents were not included in this study. It is important to study them, however, because most divorced people do eventually remarry.

In addition, future comparisons of the three custody types should include the noncustodial parent, who has been neglected by research as well as by families.

The second important research area concerns the issue of same-sex and cross-sex parenting. Given the finding of better adjustment in children living with the same-sex parent (Santrock and Warshak) along with Choderow's theoretical formulations, it would be most interesting to interview parents about this subject.

Third, investigation of the special problems of divorced black and hispanic families is long overdue, given the fact that the highest divorce rates in the country occur among nonwhites (Pope and Mueller 1976). For the sake of expediency, I was forced to limit myself to the study of white families.

Finally, there is the issue of custody for homosexual parents. Since this study began, many people have asked me for information about the adjustment of children who are awarded to gay parents. I know of only one such study, conducted by Cutrow et al. at the University of Southern California's School of Social Work. The authors reportedly found that children aged seven to twelve adjusted well to living with a lesbian mother when her partner was present.[6]

Why It Is Important that Men Mother

A colleague of mine once said that in this society, when a women achieves professional success, her male peers whisper "She's bright!" in overawed tones better reserved for dancing dogs. I do not wish to speak with equal naiveté about the fact that men can be nurturant. The following conclusions may seem to some to be a blinding glimpse of the obvious. These conclusions are addressed to those who believe that men should not raise children.

I could find no difference between the levels of functioning in households headed by fathers and mothers. The children's adjustment scores did not vary by custody. Their interactions during the family story revealed similar degrees of supportiveness. The fathers described themselves as happy and proud to be parents. These results do not "prove" that there are as many men as women who would make good parents. A selected group of men was studied. All the children in the sample, moreover, spent at least the first two years of their lives being raised by a women. These data can technically support only a modest conclusion—that, contrary to the opinion of many judges, there are *some* fathers who do make good mothers.

That men and women should feel freer than heretofore to choose the lifestyle they desire—to raise children or not—seems to be of indisputable value. Beyond the issue of greater individual freedom to choose, however, there is another reason why it is important for men to mother. It is a reason that touches on what is good for civilization as a whole. This set of issues has been analyzed and eloquently set forth by Dorothy Dinnerstein in *The Mermaid and the Minotaur*. Dinnerstein shares with Choderow a profound concern with the fact of female-dominated child care. Choderow made this issue the center of her explanation of how gender is formed in the family. Dinnerstein, however, is most concerned with understanding misogyny and relating it to the modern predicaments of our civilization.

Her argument is as follows. For the immense majority of human beings, the first "other" from whom the ego is differentiated—the first love—is a woman. This first relationship, she argues, has an intensity that no subsequent relationship can have. Indeed, at birth, the infant's relationship with the first "other" continues to be one of fusion, for the infant is not yet developed enough to distinguish its subjectivity from the mother's. Thus the symbosis with mother that exists prenatally (of necessity) continues after birth. This secondary symbiosis is *not* a biological necessity. The caring "other" could be male—or probably better still—the "others" could be both male and female.

As things are, our oldest and most deeply felt emotions—the rage and awe we feel at having been brought into this world, the love we feel for being nurtured and the terror of being left helpless, the pleasure and the agony of having to live in a mortal body—these feelings are associated with the first object, who is always a woman. It is to this set of profound and contradictory emotions that Dinnerstein ascribes the dual oppression of women throughout history—that is, of being fixed as pure and wise on the one hand and contaminating and inferior on the other.

Dinnerstein proceeds to argue that misogyny is the prototype of other forms of contempt we have for ourselves as a species. It is related to the suicidal impulse so frighteningly displayed in our atomic stockades capable of destroying all living things many times over. Misogyny is also linked to other forms of environmental destruction (that is, to the rape of "mother earth").

When men begin to share the awesome task of reproducing the species, when the infant's constellation of rage and dependency and love is directed at more than one caretaker of either sex, or both sexes, an enormous change in our evolution will have taken place.

Not only men but also women will need to change in order for equal parenting to become a reality. Recall that some of the mothers in the study felt they had a right to the custody of their children and that some joint mothers hesitated to "give up" their children three days a week to their father. In a world in which women feel powerless in the workplace, they are bound to want to maintain the power they have in the home.[7] Our notion that women are mothers and mothers are women is a part of our psychology profoundly embedded and not likely to change over night. Dinnerstein, in fact, is not at all sanguine that we will change ourselves before we destroy ourselves.

Some of us prefer optimism on principle. A civilization in which men achieve and women mother is a civilization of half-people. Any sign that people are attempting to be whole should make us look up and take notice.

Families of the Future

Joint and paternal custody seem to appear in the media more each year. Since this research began, three new guides to joint custody have appeared.[8] At the time of this writing, another state, Hawaii, has just passed a bill specifically allowing for the joint award. Judicial concern for the non-custodial parent's rights—even without joint custody—is increasingly manifest. In February of 1981, for example, New York State's highest court ruled that a custodial parent could not move out of state to pursue work because it would end the other parent's "meaningful access to the child."[9]

Increased interest in fathering, as was posited in the introduction, is certainly linked to the work of the feminist movement. The 1980s promise to be a politically conservative decade in general, and the "new right" has already begun to erode gains made in the 1970s. Some commentators believe that an interest in the reoganization of gender is a flash in the cultural pan and that the future will find us back in Ozzie and Harriet families. Such a reversal is doubtful for many reasons, but the main reason is economic. The American economy is unlikely to improve to the point where one salary will again be sufficient to sustain a family. As long as women are obliged to work, an extreme dualism between what is appropriate for the sexes is impossible.

There will indubitably be a major antifeminist backlash. Whenever an economy constricts, whenever resources are scarce, sexism and racism peak. It is impossible, however, that fathering will be forgotten completely. Not the least of the hopeful signs is that school courses entitled "Boys and Infant Care," wherein boys aged nine to twelve learn hands-on infant care, have been oversubscribed each time they were offered.[10]

As more men discover the pleasures of parenting, there will be more fathers following suit. Also, as more couples discover the convenience of joint custody, more men will be staying involved with their children after divorce. The more secure women feel in the world of work, the safer they will feel relinquishing some control of their children.

It is difficult to imagine society changing enough to support equal parenting by both sexes. It is harder still to give up hope that:

> Woman and man will start at last stably to share the credit, and stably to share the blame, for spawning mortal flesh.[11]

Notes

1. Judith Wallerstein and Joan Kelly, *Surviving the Break-up* (New York: Basic Books, 1980), p. 233.

2. Joseph Pleck, *Men's New Roles in the Family: Housework and Child Care* (Ann Arbor, Mich.: Institute for Social Research, December 1976).

3. This is the language of "Structural Family Therapy." See Salvador Minuchin, *Families and Family Therapy* (Cambridge, Mass.: Harvard University Press, 1974).

4. Lisa Cronin Wohl, "Can You Protect Your Family From The Family Protection Act?" *Ms.* 9 (1981):76-77.

5. R. Liljestrom, "The Parent's Role in Production and Reproduction," *Sweden Now* 11 (1977):73-77.

6. *National NOW Times* 14 no. 4 (1981):2.

7. For an impressive analysis of this issue, see Diane Ehrensaft, "When Women and Men Mother," *Socialist Review* 49 (1980):37-73.

8. These three excellent handbooks are: Miriam Galper's *Co-Parenting* (Philadelphia: Running Press, 1978); Mel Morgenbesser and Nadine Nehls, *Joint Custody* (Chicago: Nelson-Hall, 1981); and Isolina Ricci, *Mom's House, Dad's House* (New York: Macmillan, 1980).

9. Richard Meislin, "Court Limits Freedom Of a Divorced Parent In Choosing Residence," *New York Times,* February 25, 1981, p. A1.

10. Alison Cragin Herzig and Jane Lawrence Mali, *Oh, Boy! Babies!* (Boston: Little, Brown, 1980).

11. Dorothy Dinnerstein, *The Mermaid and the Minotaur* (New York: Harper and Row, 1976), p. 155.

Appendix A:
The Sample

The Socioeconomic Status of the Sample

Finding a measure of the socioeconomic status (SES) for this sample was a difficult problem. During the recruitment process, parents with diverse backgrounds volunteered. The question arose, "Was it reasonable to compare a single father who was a lawyer to a single mother who was a waitress?" Surely there would be differences in their problems, needs, and values that would be as much related to the difference in their social status as to the difference in their sex. The obvious solution was to match mothers and fathers on income; however, that goal created serious problems because women in the United States earn only 59 percent of men's earnings. In this sample, matching on income would have led to the matching of a father who was a forklift operator with a ninth-grade education with a mother who was a Ph.D. in history. The result would have been a sample matched on income but extremely mismatched on life experiences. It seemed more sensible to make the experimental design simulate the real-life situation as much as possible. That is, the judge, in choosing the custodial parent, decides between a father and mother who *are* in fact unmatched in income but who are fairly closely matched on educational level.

Thus education was selected as the indicator of social status. The sixteen mothers and sixteen fathers were divided into a high-education group (that is, B.A. or more) and a low-education group (that is, two years of college or less). The joint families were not matched in this way because they were too scarce. All the joint parents had college degrees except for parents Y and Z, who had completed four or fewer years of high school (tables A-1 through A-4).

Table A-1

Mean Years Since Final Separation, Mean Age of Parents, and Religion, by Custody

Custody	n	Years since Separation	Age of Parent	Religion (%)
Mothers	16	3.84	37.1	Catholic, 37 Protestant, 50 Quaker, 6 Jewish, 6
Fathers	16	3.4	37.2	Catholic, 37 Protestant, 50 Mormon, 12
Joint mothers[a]	9	3.38	36.5	Catholic, 22 Protestant, 66 Jewish, 11
Joint fathers	9	3.61	37	Catholic, 11 Protestant, 77 Jewish, 11

Notes: Mean years since final separation was independent of custody. $F(3, 46) = .08$; $p > .10$. There was no significant difference on age by custody. $F(3, 46) = .02$; $p > .10$.

The proportions of Protestants, Catholics, and Jews within each custody type did not differ from the proportions of these religions in the sample. $X^2(3) = 4.37$; $p > .10$.

[a]There were seven joint cases in which both parents participated in the study. In addition, there were two joint mothers and two joint fathers whose ex-spouses did *not* participate. This resulted in a sample of nine joint mothers and nine joint fathers.

Table A-2
Percentage of Maternal-, Paternal-, and Joint-Custody Children Belonging to a Given Age Bracket

	Custody Type		
Age[a]	Maternal	Paternal	Joint
Preschool			
(2-6 years)	8%	9%	24%
n	(3)	(3)	(6)
Latency			
(7-10 years)	26%	31%	36%
n	(9)	(10)	(9)
Preadolescent			
(11-12)	15%	13%	24%
n	(5)	(4)	(6)
Teens			
(13+)	50%	46%	16%
n	(17)	(15)	(4)
	100%	100%	100%
Total n	34	32	25
Mean age	12 years	11 years	9.5 years

[a]At the time of the interview.

Table A-3
Number of Families Recruited from Various Sources, by Custody Type

	Recruitment Source				
Custody Type[a]	Singles Groups	Newspaper Advertisements	Other Sources	Colleagues	Total
Fathers	50%	—	37%	12%	100%
(n)	(8)	—	(6)	(2)	16
Mothers	44%	25%	12%	19%	100%
(n)	(7)	(4)	(2)	(3)	16
Joint mothers	11%	22%	33%	33%	100%
(n)	(1)	(2)	(3)	(3)	9
Joint fathers	11%	—	44%	44%	100%
(n)	(1)	—	(4)	(4)	9

[a]The recruitment sources of the paternal and joint families differs significantly from those of single custody mothers. $X^2(9) = 37.37$; $p < .001$.

Table A-4
Definition of Five Visitation Arrangements

Type of Visitation	*Amount of Contact*
I None	
II Rare	a. One day every other month, or b. 1-3 times per year for one week.
III Occasional	a. Once per month for a weekend or less, or b. Once per three weeks for a week-end or less.
IV Frequent	a. Every other week for a few hours, or b. every other week for a day, or c. every other week for a weekend, or d. once per week for a half-day, or e. once per week for a day.
V Continuous	a. Two full days per week, or b. full weekends plus frequent short visits during the week.

Appendix B:
Statistical Results

Table B-1
Mean Piers-Harris Self-Concept Scores by Custody Type and Parental Conflict

	Parental Conflict[a]	
Custody[b]	High	Low
Maternal	52.83	64.69
Paternal	53.87	63.82
Joint	60.5	63.00

[a]$F(1, 66) = 4.15; p < .05.$
[b]$F(2, 66) = .20; p > .25$ ns.

Table B-2
Parents' Ratings of Children's Adjustment by Custody Type

Measure	Custody	X	SD	(df)/F
Psychosomatic problems[a]	Maternal	.852	1.36	(2, 85)
	Paternal	.72	1.67	.433
	Joint	.62	1.07	ns*
Behavior problems[b]	Maternal	2.94	4.38	(2, 85)
	Paternal	2.28	2.66	1.66
	Joint	2.25	2.9	ns*
Self-esteem[c]	Maternal	13.79	3.73	(2, 85)
	Paternal	14.46	2.66	.423
	Joint	14.42	3.48	ns*

[a]Low scores mean few problems.
[b]Low scores mean few problems.
[c]High scores mean high esteem.
*$p > .10.$

Table B-3
Parents' Ratings of Children's Adjustment, by Conflict

| Adjustment Measure | Parental Conflict | |
	High	Low
Esteem[a]	X = 13.08	X = 14.89
	SD = 3.04	SD = 3.10
	$F(1, 85)$ = 7.43*	
Behavior problems[b]	X = 4.31	X = 2.03
	SD = 4.4	SD = 2.6
	$F(1, 85)$ = 9.70*	
Psychosomatic problems[c]	X = 1.27	X = 0.492
	SD = 2.0	SD = 1.04
	$F(1, 85)$ = 11.62*	

[a]High scores mean high esteem.
[b]Low scores mean few problems.
[c]Low scores mean few problems.
*$p < .001$.

Table B-4
The Rank-Stress Scale
Parents were asked to rank nine items from 1-9 according to how stressful they were. The average rankings were as follows.

High-Education Mothers	*Low-Education Mothers*
1. Money	1. Money
2. Having both to work and care for children	2. Feeling totally responsible for children
3. Loneliness	3. Loneliness
4. Feeling totally responsible for children	4. Having both to work and care for children
5. Disciplining	5. Dealing with ex
6. Dealing with ex	6. Stigma
7. Cleaning	7. Disciplining
8. Stigma	8. Cooking
9. Cooking	9. Cleaning

High-Education Fathers	*Low-Education Fathers*
1. Loneliness	1. Loneliness
2. Feeling totally responsible for children	2. Feeling totally responsible for children
3. Money	3. Having both to work and care for children
4. Having both to work and care for children	4. Money
5. Dealing with ex	5. Dealing with ex
6. Disciplining	6. Disciplining
7. Cleaning	7. Cleaning
8. Cooking	8. Cooking
9. Stigma	9. Stigma

Joint Mothers	*Joint Fathers*
1. Money	1. Loneliness
2. Loneliness	2. Money
3. Having both to work and care for children	3. Having both to work and care for children
4. Dealing with ex	4. Dealing with ex
5. Disciplining	5. Feeling totally responsible for children
6. Feeling totally responsible for children	6. Disciplining
7. Cleaning	7. Cooking
8. Stigma	8. Cleaning
9. Cooking	9. Stigma

Appendix C:
Research Instruments

Parents' Ratings of Children

Parents were asked to rate each child's psychosomatic and behavior problems on the following scale: 1 = a problem that is mild in intensity and acute in occurrence; 2 = a problem that is mild in intensity and chronic in occurrence; 2 = also a problem that is severe in intensity and acute in occurrence; and 3 = a problem that is both severe and chronic.

Psychosomatic Problems

Parents were asked to rate the following problems for each child on the scale just described. The numbers were added to give a "psychosomatic score."

Allergies	Eating problems
Asthma	Ulcers
Colitis	Headaches
Epilepsy	Sleeping problems

(Possible scores range from 0-27.)

Behavior Problems

Temper tantrums	Aggression
Sadness, withdrawal	Lying
Irritability	Stealing
Fearfulness, anxiety	Cheating

(Possible scores range from 0-24.)

Self-Esteem

Parents rated their children on the following questions on a scale from 1-5, that is, never, rarely, sometimes, often, always:

1. Does he or she lack self-confidence in abilities?
2. Does he or she show extreme sensitivity to teasing or criticism?
3. Does this child feel good about himself or herself?
4. Does he or she need more reassurance than most children?

The TAT Family-Interaction Task—Procedures and Coding Manual

Procedures

The entire family was asked to sit together, after which the examiner (*E*) presented them with a TAT card and the following directions:

> I'd like you to tell a story about what you think is happening in the picture. Try and decide who the people might be, what they might be doing and feeling, and what will happen in the end. There are no right or wrong answers. People see different things when they look at the cards. It is very important that you work together to create the story. Do not make up four individual stories. Rather, help to give each other ideas and make one story together.

The family could spend as much time as they wished on a given card. After they had completed their story, *E* offered them the second card. This procedure continued until the fifth card.

Instead of relying on the condenser microphone, the extension microphone was used so that the family would have another important item to negotiate. Deciding who was to hold the microphone and for how long enabled them to demonstrate their ability to cooperate.

The following coding system was based on Alexander's (1973) system. Because he was working with videotape and also because his manual is not thorough, it was necessary to elaborate a scheme that would fit the needs of this task.

This coding scheme has nothing to do with content. It was completely irrelevant whether the family told stories about death or days in the park. Only their interactions were coded.

The realm of possible interactions has been divided into two categories: supportive and nonsupportive. Any behavior that enhanced the collaborative performance of the task was considered supportive. Behavior that disrupted or subverted the family's collaboration was considered nonsupportive. Each category was divided into several subcategories, as described below.

Supportive Responses

Confirmation.

1.   Any statement of validation, for example, "That's an interesting idea" or "You're so good at this!"

2. Any attempt to ask a question about or to reflect the feeling of another person, for example, "Does that picture make you sad?" or "You look like you're enjoying this."
3. Any restatement by one person of another's response with the intent of encouraging that person, for example, "I think it's a farm family." "Oh, you think it's a farm family." The second statement is confirming the value of the first.

Equality.

1. Always refers to the attempt to distribute fairly power or resources, for example, the airwaves, possession of the microphone or the card. Examples: "Why don't we take turns so each one can hold the mike," or "I've held the card a lot; would you like to hold it?"
2. When one person has spoken and either that person or someone else acts to shift the floor to another speaker with the intent to include her or him, this is equality. Examples: One person has been talking, and mother says, "How about you, Bobby? Do you agree with that?" or "I've been talking a lot. What do you think, Dad?"
3. A statement that does the opposite of pulling rank. Example: When a parent says to the children, "Wow. These are hard for me, too," or "Your ideas are as good as mine."
4. All teasing is in this category, unless it is clearly nasty. Example: "Look at that guy's gray hair. He looks like you, Dad." Teasing always assumes that one has—or at least temporarily assumes—equal status.

Information Giving or Seeking. This category includes any statement or question that does not come under the other categories. Examples are: "I think it's a horse." "What do you think the boy has?" "Maybe it's a mouse." "A what?" "I agree." "I disagree." "Yes." "No." Each of these is coded as one instance of information giving or seeking. This behavior is considered supportive because it reflects the family's ability to collaborate to accomplish a task.

Conflict Resolution. If two people are fighting over a power issue, for example, who will hold the microphone, a conflict-resolving answer would be, "We could take turns." This would be equality if it were not preceded by a conflict.

Nonsupportive Responses

Indifference. Messages that indicate that a person is bored such as, "I don't want to do this," would be coded as indifference. Of if a person turns to another to say, "Do you agree this is a sad boy?" and the person returns an apathetic, "Sure," this would also be coded as "indifference."

Unilateral Control

1. Any seizure of power, for example, a child grabbing the microphone in the middle of a story to sing.
2. Fighting, for example, two people struggling over the mike.
3. Any time someone wanders off, that is, leaves the task to do something else. Usually this is a child who has taken off for a toy to see if the parent will call him back.

Attack. Any negative evaluation of a person or their behavior, for example, "You act like an idiot."

Invalidation. This also deals with negative evaluation, but it takes the form of replacing someone's idea with one's own. It is an attempt to disqualify the competence of another person, for example, "I've done these things a hundred times; I ought to know," or "That's not a cat, it's a baby, you fool."

Laughter. (This category was coded, but it was not counted in the family's final scores.) Laughter was tallied in its own column, except for two types that were included in the preceding categories: (1) The *controlling giggle*, as when a child grabs the mike and laughs into it, (2) when someone laughs nervously, for example, because she or he feels self-conscious. The first example was coded as "control" and the second was not coded.

Examiner's Responses. (This category was coded, but it was not counted in the family's final scores.) People almost always asked *E* questions during the task. Their questions were coded as information seeking (unless it was clearly control or something else). *E*'s response was also tallied. This was done to make sure *E* had not offered more help to one custody group than to another.

Coding the Tapes

The most important rule in coding a given statement was to listen both to the message and the metamessage. The *metamessage* is the constellation of nonverbal and contextual clues that transform the meaning of words as they are spoken. For example, the response, "Does this card make you feel sad?" would probably be coded as "confirmation," as long as it was said sincerely. It would be possible to say the same words in a sarcastic or threatening way. Whenever there appeared to be a discrepancy between the literal message and the metamessage, the latter was coded. This, of course, makes the task more complex and detracts from the usefulness of a manual like this. As language is a social phenomenon, however, it would have been meaningless to code for content alone.

Mechanics. Two coders worked simultaneously on the tapes. It was necessary for one to turn on the recorder and to stop it every five seconds. The coders then silently rated the segment. That is, they might have heard one parental "confirmation" and two child "information seekings." The reason the work was done simultaneously was that one coder could not give the tape to another and expect that she could start timing exactly at the moment the first coder did. A discrepancy of even one second would set the entire process off.

A coding sheet was made and divided into parent responses and children responses. (The children were lumped together because a coder who had never seen the children in person could never distinguish three young voices on tape.) Then each category (that is, parent and child) was divided into supportive and nonsupportive responses. Then each of these was divided into the subgroups outlined here (for example, confirmation and equality).

Scoring. The final scoring was: the total number of supportive responses (parents plus children) minus the total number of nonsupportive responses, all divided by the number of five-second intervals they used for the task.

A coder, blind to the hypotheses, was trained for six weeks on practice tapes until 96 percent agreement with E was reached. Subsequently, every tenth tape coded was checked with E, and agreement stayed between 88 percent and 95 percent. ANOVA was used to test differences among the scores by custody.

The TAT Cards. The cards used were 13B, 2, 7BM, 18GF, and 7GF and were presented in that order. They were chosen because they draw themes of family life and include both sexes.

Interview Schedule: Parents' Interview

Demographics, Custody, and Visitation

1. How long were you married?
2. When was the final separation? The divorce?

3. What were the grounds for the divorce? Was it contested?
4. How old are you?
5. How much education have you had?
6. What is your occupation?
7. What is your religion?
8. How did you decide you should have custody?
9. What were your reasons for wanting custody?
10. Describe any conflict you had with ex over custody.
11. Did your ex ever desire custody?
12. Did you consider seriously letting ex have custody?
13. Why did you consider it, and why did you decide against it?
14. Have you ever heard of joint custody? Did you consider it?
15. Why did you decide against joint custody?
16. Did you consult with anyone (for example, lawyer, friends, psychologist, clergy) on the question of custody?
17. What type of help did this person give you?
18. Did you consult the children at all about custody?
19. How did you handle this? If you did not consult them, why not?
20. For joint parents: Where did you first hear about joint custody? Did anyone try to talk you out of joint custody? Explain.
21. Describe the joint arrangement you have in detail. When do children go to the other house?
22. As a joint parent, which decisions do you make with your ex? Give examples. How did making decisions together work?
23. Do you feel the best custody decision was made? Explain.
24. Have you ever regretted this decision? Explain.
25. What are the advantages of this form of custody?
26. What are the disadvantages of this form of custody?
27. What was the legal visitation agreement?
28. What is the actual visitation situation?
29. What are the reasons for the discrepancy?
30. Did you consult anyone on the question of visitation? What type of help did that person offer?
31. How satisfied are you with present visitation levels?
32. Would you rather your ex saw the children more or less? Why?
33. Do the children enjoy the visits?
34. How do you feel when you see your ex?
35. Do you see or speak to your ex when she or he comes to pick up the children?

Predivorce Conflict

36. What was the atmosphere like in your home before the divorce? (1) mostly

tranquil; (2) we fought but children didn't know; (3) tense but no fighting; (4) half tranquil, half turbulent; (5) mostly turbulent.

37. How often was there a fight, considering now your entire marriage? (7) several times a day; (6) daily; (5) several times a week; (4) weekly; (3) several times a month; (2) monthly; (1) several times a year; (0) not at all.

38. Considering the worst time in your relationship in the marriage, how often did you fight: (same scale as above).

39. How often would you say the tension level was high during that last period? never = 1; rarely = 2; sometimes = 3; often = 4; always = 5.

40. Did you fight in front of the children? N, R, S, O, A (as above).

41. Did physical violence ever occur? N, R, S, O, A.

42. Did it occur in front of children? N, R, S, O, A.

43. Were children aware of the violence, even if they did not see it? N, R, S, O, A.

(Scores range from 6-44.)

Postdivorce Conflict

44. Do you still fight with your ex? (Same scale as no. 35 above.)

45. Is there more or less fighting than before the divorce? Much less = 1; less = 2; same = 3; more = 4; much more = 5.

46. Do you fight in front of children now? N, R, S, O, A (1-5).

47. Does physical violence occur between you and ex? N, R, S, O, A.

48. Does it occur in front of children? N, R, S, O, A.

49. Are children aware of it, even if they do not see it? N, R, S, O, A.

50. How often is the tension high between you and your ex? N, R, S, O, A.

51. Do you find yourself talking against ex to children? N, R, S, O, A.

(Scores range from 7-42.)

Family Functions

A. Authority

1. Who does most of the disciplining of the children now?

2. Who did it before the divorce?

3. Why doesn't your ex do more disciplining? Have you discussed this with ex? Explain.

4. Has your style of disciplining changed (for example, stricter or more lenient)? Why? Give an example.

5. What are the problems of disciplining as a custodial parent?

6. Do you feel two parents could handle them better? Why?
7. Do you feel a man or woman could discipline them better? Why?
8. Do they play you and your ex off each other? Describe.
9. Are they harder to handle when they come back from a visit? Describe.
10. Is solo disciplining overwhelming? Why?
11. Joint parents: Are there two sets of rules in each house for the children? Give examples.
12. Do children seem confused by these rules? Give example.
13. Do children play you off? Describe.
14. Has joint custody increased or decreased problems caused by the different styles of discipline you and your ex had?
15. Are there any advantages to being the custodial disciplinarian? (Or the joint disciplinarian?) Describe.

B. Housekeeping

1. Do you do more, less, or the same housekeeping as before?
2. What accounts for the change?
3. How do you feel about doing more or less?
4. Do you have paid help? Did you have it before?
5. Do children do more work now?
6. What are children's feelings about doing more work? What are your feelings about it?
7. What are the problems of running the house alone?
8. Did you have to learn any new things? What were they?
9. Who taught you the new skills (repairing, painting, and so on)?
10. Did you enjoy it, or was it stressful?
11. Do you rely on any other people in your life to do household things your ex once did (for example, cooking, laundry, driving, repairs, and shopping)? How do you feel about receiving such help?
12. Are there any advantages to being totally responsible for the house? Explain.

C. Economics

1. Is your income adequate for your needs? $N = 5, R = 4, S = 3, O = 2, A = 1$. (Answer same question for before the divorce.)
2. Is money a major worry in your life? $N = 1, R = 2, S = 3, O = 4. A = 5$. (Answer same question for before the divorce.)
3. Do your ex-spouse's support payments come reliably? Explain.
4. Have you ever gone back to court to fight for support or alimony? (If not awarded alimony or support, why not?)
5. What are the money-related problems you have as a single parent?

6. Did you have to move for financial reasons?
7. What were your feelings about moving?
8. Has the new residence brought any new problems? Describe.
9. Did you go out to work for the first time? Describe.
10. Did you change jobs or hours because of having custody? Describe.
11. Do you have more or less money than while you were married? Why?
12. Had you managed and budgeted money before the divorce? If not, was this difficult to learn?
13. Are there any advantages to being totally responsible for the family's income? Explain.

D. Child Care

1. Has your child ever been in the custody of your ex?
2. Why? Describe duration and reasons for change.
3. How did the child react to the switch?
4. Has your child ever been in substitute daycare—either at a daycare center or with a sitter?
5. How old was the child?
6. For how long was (s)he in substitute care? For how many hours per week?
7. What are the problems of finding substitute care?
8. Will your child have experienced more substitute care because of the divorce than he or she would have otherwise? How do you feel about that?
9. How do you feel about the quality of care he or she receives?
10. Does the child seem to like that caretaker(s)?
11. Do you use more evening substitute care than you did as a married parent? Why?
12. Is it difficult to get sitters? Explain.
13. Do you have more, less, or the same amount of contact with your children as you had during the marriage? Describe.
14. How do you feel about this change in contact?
15. Do you feel closer, less close, or the same closeness with your children? Why is this the case?
16. Are there any advantages to being more responsible for child-care functions? Describe.

E. Support Systems

Describe the support group that you had before the divorce. In other words, whom did you count on for love and for help of any kind, for example, with loaning money, listening to problems, and doing favors.

Now describe your support group as it exists today.

1. Why has this change come about?
2. How do you feel about the difference? Is there any overlap between your pre- and postdivorce support groups?
3. Do you date now? Any reason why not?
4. How often do you date?
5. Do you try to date without your children's knowing about or meeting your dates? Why?
6. How do your children feel about your going out?
7. Does the presence of the children inhibit your dating behavior in any way? Describe.
8. Are your parents living? Where?
9. How often did you see parents before divorce?
10. How often do you see them now?
11. What is the reason for the change?
12. How do you feel about the change?
13. What functions do your relatives play in your life: for example, confiding and caring, loaning or giving money, babysitting, repairs, and moving?
14. How do you feel about accepting help from them? Has this brought about any new problems?
15. Stigma: Do you feel you are treated differently as a divorced parent from when you were married? By whom?
16. Are you invited out as much as you were before, to dinner parties, and so on?
17. Do you have trouble getting a sitter as a divorced parent?
18. Have you ever had problems with credit, landlords, employers, or the church because of your divorced status? Describe.

Interview Schedule: Children's Interview

Warm-Up Questions

1. How old are you?
2. What grade are you in? (Or) Do you go to daycare?
3. Do you like it? Do you like your teacher?
4. What is your favorite subject?

Background of the Divorce

1. Where does your noncustodial parent live?
2. Why did your parents get divorced?
3. Whose fault was it?

4. Who told you about the divorce? What did that person say? Did he or she explain it well? Were you confused? Are you still confused? In what way?

5. Do you think your parents will get back together again? Do you wish they would? Did you wish they would get back together when you were little?

Reactions to the Divorce

1. How did you feel when you found out about the divorce? For example, were you surprised? Why? Sad? About what? Worried? Explain. Angry? At whom? Explain. Happy? Why? Afraid? Of what?

Custody

1. Did your parents ask you with whom you wanted to live? If yes, was it hard to choose? Why? Whom did you choose? Why did you want to be with that parent? Are you glad they did ask you, or do you wish they wouldn't have? If no, do you wish they would have asked you? Why or why not? Whom would you have said if they had asked you? Would it have been hard to choose?

2. Are you glad you live with whom you do? Do you get along well?

3. Do you ever wish you lived with your other parent? Why?

4. Would you prefer to switch custodians now, if they asked you? Why?

Visitation/Joint-Custody Lifestyle

1. When do you see your other parent? Is that enough? Would you like to see him or her more or less? A lot more or a lot less? Same?

2. What do you do when you are with your other parent?

3. Is it fun?

4. Do you have to do any chores over there? Do you do more chores in this house or that one?

5. Can you have a heart-to-heart talk with the parent you live with? With the other one?

6. Do you ever miss the other parent? For what? What do you do when you start to miss them?

7. Do Mom and Dad have different rules? Say, about bedtimes, TV, chores, homework, friends, and so on? Give an example. Is it ever confusing to have two sets of rules to follow? Give an example. What did you do about it?

8. For joint-custody children only: What is it like living in two houses? What are the problems? Do you forget things at one house? What happens then? Do you like one house better? Why? Is it ever confusing to have to move back and forth? Why? Is there anything nice about living

in two houses? Would you prefer to live this way, or just to live with one parent and visit the other? Why?

(If the child has ever been in a different custody situation: When did you live with your other parent? What was that like? How did you feel about switching? Do you like this arrangement better or worse? Why?)

Predivorce Parental Conflict

1. When your parents were married, did they fight a lot? A little bit? Never?
2. How did you feel when they fought? What would you do?
3. What was it like in your house—mostly nice? Mostly fights? Half and Half?
4. Did they fight in front of you? A lot? A little? Never?

Postdivorce Parental Conflict

1. Do your parents still fight? A lot? A little? Never?
2. Do they fight more or less or the same as before?
3. Do they fight in front of you? What do you do then?
4. Does one parent say bad things about the other? Who? What do you do when this happens?

Family Functions

A. Authority

1. Is your custodial parent stricter now than before the divorce?
2. In what ways?
3. Who is stricter now, Mom or Dad? In what ways?

B. Domestics

1. Which chores do you have now?
2. Is that more or less than before the divorce?
3. Do you feel you do more because there is only one parent?
4. How do you feel about that?

C. Economics

1. Did you move after the divorce? Do you like your new house?
2. How did you feel about leaving the old neighborhood—more sad or more glad?

D. Child Care

    1. Does your custodian go out more, or did he or she go out more before the divorce? How do you feel about that? Do you wish he or she would stay home more?

    2. Who stays with you when he or she goes out? Do you like that sitter?

    3. Do you spend as much time with your parent as you would like to? Why not? Have you made your wishes known? With what result?

    4. Do you feel as close to each of your parents as you did before the divorce? Explain.

E. Support Systems

    1. Who helped you through the divorce? How did they help?

    2. Since the divorce, have you become closer to any other adults such as teachers, relatives, or neighbors? Describe.

    3. Does your parent lean on you for support? How do you feel about this? In what way does he or she rely on you?

Stigma

1. Do your friends know about the divorce?

2. Is it ever embarrassing when someone finds out? Explain.

3. Did anyone ever treat you differently because of the divorce, for example, tease you or act sympathetic? Describe.

Effects on Child

1. Did your grades go up or down because of the divorce—either before or after it? Why did this happen? Are you doing better now than before the divorce? Why?

2. How did the divorce affect you, for example, did you get depressed? Did you feel angry all the time? Did you start to do more bad things? Describe. How long did that last?

References

Aguilera, D., and Messick, J. 1974. *Crisis intervention: Theory and methodology.* Saint Louis: Mosby.

Ahern, D., and Bliss, B. 1976. *The economics of being a woman.* New York: McGraw-Hill.

Ahrons, C. 1979. The binuclear family: Two households, one family. *Alternative Lifestyles* 2, no. 4:499-515.

Alexander, J. 1973. Defensive and supportive communications in normal and deviant families. *Journal of Consulting and Clinical Psychology* 40:223-231.

Bateson, G. 1979. *Mind and nature.* New York: Dutton.

Bettelheim, B. 1956. Fathers shouldn't try to be mothers. *Parents' Magazine*, October, pp. 124-125.

Bloom, B.L. 1978. Marital disruption as a stressor: A review and an analysis. *Psychological Bulletin* 85:867-894.

Bowlby, J. 1969. *Attachment and loss, vol. I: Attachment.* New York: Basic Books.

Braiman v. *Braiman.* 1978. 44 N.Y. 2nd 584, 407 N.Y.S. 2nd 449, 378 N.E. 2nd 1019.

Brandwein, R., Brown, C., and Fox, E. 1974. Women and children last: The social situation of divorced mothers and their families. *Journal of Marriage and the Family* 36:498-514.

Broverman, I., Broverman, D., Clarkson, F. Rosenkrantz, P., and Vogel, S. 1970. Sex-role stereotypes and clinical judgments of mental health. *Journal of Consulting and Clinical Psychology* 34:1-7.

Castro, F. 1974. *The revolution has in Cuban women today an impressive political force.* Havana: Editorial de Ciencias Sociales.

Choderow, N. 1978. *The reproduction of mothering.* Berkeley: University of California Press.

Cooper, D. 1971. *The death of the family.* New York: Vintage Books.

Corman, A. 1977. *Kramer versus Kramer.* New York: New American Library.

Cutrow, M., Hoppman, P., and Lehman, J. 1981. *National Now Times* 14:2.

Dodson, F. 1974. *How to father.* New York: New American Library.

Ehrenreich, B. 1979. How to get housework out of your system. *Ms.* 8:47-80.

Ehrensaft, D. 1980. When women and men mother. *Socialist Review* 49: 37-73.

Erikson, E. 1950. *Childhood and society.* New York: Norton.

Etaugh, C. 1980. Effects of nonmaternal care on children. *American Psychologist* 35:309-319.

Finlay v. *Finlay*. 1925. 148 N.E. at 626.

Foster, H. 1973. Adoption and child custody: Best interests of the child? *Buffalo Law Review* 22:1-16.

Foster, H., and Freed, D. 1980. Joint custody. *Trial*, June, pp. 22-27.

Friedan, B. 1963. *The feminine mystique*. New York: Dell.

Galbraith, J.K. 1973. *Economics and the public purpose*. Boston: Houghton Mifflin.

Galper, M. 1978. *Co-parenting*. Philadelphia: Running Press.

Gersick, K. 1979. Fathers by choice: Divorced men who receive custody of their children. In G. Levininger and O. Moles, eds., *Divorce and separation*. New York: Basic Books.

Glick, P.C. 1979. Children of divorced parents in demographic perspective. *Journal of Social Issues* 35, no. 4:170-182.

Goldstein, J., Freud, A., and Solnit, A. 1979. *Before the best interests of the child*. New York: Free Press.

Goldstein, J., Freud, A., and Solnit, A. 1973. *Beyond the best interests of the child*. New York: Free Press.

Greif, J.B. 1979. Fathers, children and joint custody. *American Journal of Orthopsychiatry* 49:311-319.

Harlow, H.F., Harlow, M.K., Dodsworth, R.O., and Arling, G.L. 1970. Maternal behavior of rhesus monkeys deprived of mothering and peer associations in infants. In Freda Rebelsky, ed., *Child Development and Behavior*. New York: Knopf, pp, 88-98.

Herzig, A.C., and Mali, J.L. 1980. *Oh, Boy! Babies*. Boston: Little, Brown.

Herzog, E., and Sudia, C. 1973. Children in fatherless families. In B. Caldwell and H.N. Ricciuti, eds., *Review of child development research*, vol. 3. Chicago: University of Chicago Press.

Hess, R.D., and Camara, K.A. 1979. Post-divorce family relationships as mediating factors in the consequences of divorce for children. *Journal of Social Issues* 35, no. 4:79-97.

Hetherington, M., Cox, M., and Cox, R. 1976. Divorced fathers. *The Family Coordinator*, October, pp. 417-426.

——— . 1979. Play and social interaction in children following divorce. *Journal of Social Issues* 35, no. 4:26-49.

Hofferth, S. 1979. Daycare in the next decade: 1980-1990. *Journal of Marriage and the Family*, August, pp. 649-657.

Irving, J. 1979. *The world according to Garp*. New York: Simon and Schuster.

James, H. 1979. *What Maisie knew*. New York: Penguin Books.

Jens, K. 1976. Field studies of the coping process: A review. Unpublished manuscript, Department of Psychology, State University of New York at Buffalo.

Kalter, N. 1977. Children of divorce in an outpatient psychiatric population. *American Journal of Orthopsychiatry* 47:40-51.

Katkin, D., Bullington, B., and Levine, M. 1974. Above and beyond the best interests of the child: An inquiry into the relationship between social science and social action. *Law and Society Review*, Summer, pp. 669-689.

Kelly, J., and Wallerstein, J. 1976. The effects of parental divorce: Experiences of the child in early latency. *American Journal of Orthopsychiatry* 46:20-32.

Klein, Ted. 1968. *Father and child*. New York: William Morrow.

Lamb, M. 1977. Father-infant and mother-infant interaction in the first year of life. *Child Development* 48:167-181.

Lasch, C. 1979. *The culture of narcissism*. New York: Norton.

Levine, J. 1976. *Who will raise the children?* New York: Lippincott.

Liljestrom, R. 1977. The parent's role in production and reproduction. *Sweden Now* 11:73-77.

Luepnitz, D.A. 1978. Children of divorce: A review of the psychological literature. *Law and Human Behavior* 2:167-179.

_____. 1979. Which aspects of divorce affect children? *The Family Coordinator* 28:79-86.

_____. 1981. A review of Wallerstein and Kelly's, *Surviving the Break-Up. Journal of Marriage and the Family* November 1981.

Maccoby, E., and Jacklin, C. 1974. *The psychology of sex differences*. Stanford, Calif.: Stanford University Press.

McDermott, J.F. 1970. Divorce and its psychiatric sequelae in children. *Archives of General Psychiatry* 23:421-428.

Mainardi, P. 1970. The politics of housework. In L. Tanner, ed., *Voices from women's liberation*. New York: New American Library.

Meislin, R. 1981. Court limits freedom of a divorced parent in choosing residence. *New York Times*, February 25, p. A1.

Minuchin, S. 1974. *Families and family therapy*. Cambridge: Harvard University Press.

Morgenbesser, M., and Nehls, N. 1981. *Joint Custody*. Chicago: Nelson-Hall.

Morrison, T. 1977. *Song of Solomon*. New York: New American Library.

National NOW Times. 1981. *14* (4).

Parsons, T., and Bales, R. 1955. *Family, socialization and interaction process*. New York: Free Press.

People v. *Mecein*. 1839. 8 Paige Ch. 46, 69.

Phillips v. *Phillips*. 1943. 153 Florida, 133, 13 So 2d 922.

Pleck, J. 1976. *Men's new roles in the family: Housework and child care*. Ann Arbor, Mich.: Institute for Social Research, December.

Pope, H., and Mueller, C.W. 1976. The intergenerational transmission of marital instability: Comparisons by race and sex. *Journal of Social Issues* 32:49-66.

Poster, M. 1978. *Critical theory of the family.* New York: Seabury Press.

Raschke, H., and Raschke, V. 1979. Family conflict and children's self-concepts: A comparison of intact and single-parent families. *Journal of Marriage and the Family* 41, no. 2:367-374.

Ricci, I. 1980. *Mom's house, Dad's house.* New York: Macmillan.

Robinson, L. 1978. *Sex, class and culture.* Bloomington: Indiana University Press.

Roman, M., and Haddad, W. 1978. *The disposable parent.* New York: Holt, Reinhart and Winston.

Rosenthal, K., and Keshet, H. 1981. *Fathers without partners.* Totowa, N.J.: Roman & Littlefield.

Rossi, A. 1977. A biosocial perspective on parenting. *Daedalus,* Spring pp. 1-31.

Rubin, L. 1976 *Worlds of pain: Life in the working class family.* New York: Basic Books.

Rutter, M. 1971. Parent-child separation: Psychological effects on the children. *Journal of Child Psychology and Psychiatry* 12:233-260.

Salk, L. 1978. *What every child would like his parents to know about divorce.* New York: Warner Books.

Santrock, J., and Tracy, R. 1978. Effects of children's family structure status on the development of stereotypes in teachers. *Journal of Educational Psychology,* 70:754-757.

Santrock, J., and Warshak, R. 1979. Father custody and social development in boys and girls. *Journal of Social Issues* 35, no. 4:112-125.

Shinn, M.B. 1978. Father absence and children's cognitive development. *Psychological Bulletin* 85:295-324.

Spock, B. 1974. *Raising children in a difficult time.* New York: Norton.

Stack, C. 1976. Who owns the child? Divorce and custody decisions in middle-class families. *Social Problems* 23:505-515.

Swedish Institute. 1977. *Social Benefits in Sweden.* Stockholm: Trygg Hansa.

Tooley, K. 1976. Anti-social behavior and social alienation post-divorce: The man of the house and his myth. *American Journal of Orthopsychiatry* 46:33-42.

Tuckman, J., and Regan, R. 1966. Intactness of home and behavioral problems in children. *Journal of Child Psychology and Psychiatry* 7:225-233.

U.S. Bureau of the Census. 1977. *Statistical abstract of the United States.* Washington, D.C.: Government Printing Office.

_____ . 1977. *Projections of the population of the United States: 1977-2050.* (Current Population Reports, Series P-25, No. 704). Washington, D.C.: Government Printing Office.

U.S. Bureau of Labor Statistics. 1978. *Marital and family characteristics of workers*, March 1977. (Special Labor Force Report 216.) Washington, D.C.: Government Printing Office.

Van Gelder, L. 1981. Single mothers—Last of the supermoms. *Ms.*, April, pp. 47-50.

Wallerstein, J., and Kelly, J. 1980. *Surviving the break-up*. New York: Basic Books.

Weiss, R.S. 1979. *Going it alone*. New York: Basic Books.

_____. 1973. Helping relationships of clients with physicians, social workers, priests and others. *Social Problems* 20:319-328.

_____. 1968. Issues in holistic research. In H.S. Becker, B. Geer, D. Riesman, and R.S. Weiss, eds., *Institutions and the person*. Chicago: Aldine.

_____. 1975. *Marital separation*. New York: Basic Books.

_____. 1978. The adjudication of custody when parents separate. Unpublished paper, excerpted in G. Levininger and O. Moles, eds., *Divorce and separation*. New York: Basic Books, 1979.

World Health Organization Expert Committee on Mental Health. 1951. Report of the Second Session. Technical Report Series No. 31. Geneva: World Health Organization.

Wohl, L.C. 1981. Can you protect your family from the Family Protection Act? *Ms.* 9:76-77.

Woolf, V. 1963. *Three guineas*. New York: Harcourt, Brace and World.

Index

Ahrons, Constance, 13
Alimony, and fathers, 58-59; and mothers, 57-58; waiving, 73
Annulments, 131-132

Bateson, G., 14, 15, 21
Bettelheim, B., 1
Bloom, B., 146
Broverman et al., 9

California, joint custody law in, 4
Childcare, 111-122; analysis of female-dominated, 8-11, 155-157; use of substitute, 112-116
Children, adjustment of, 18-19, 149-150, 152; effects of divorce on, 4-8; limit-testing of, 85-88, 91-94; opinions about custody, 32-33, 46-48; opinions about visitation, 35-37
Child support, 56-58, 67-70
Choderow, N., 10-11, 156
Conflict, parental, and discipline, 86, 89-90, 91-93; effects on children, 7-8, 149; and joint custody, 17, 19, 149
Cooking, and joint custody, 106; and fathers, 99, 101-103, 108-110; and mothers, 99
Coping, defined, 103
Counseling (see Therapy)
Crisis theory, 16, 21
Critical theory, 15, 16, 153
Cuba, female-dominated childcare in, 9; sharing domestic labor in, 109
Custody, anxiety over losing, 31-32; children's satisfaction with, 32-33, 46-48; consulting children on, 26-28; history of, 2-4; how parents decided on, 23-26; 38-42; parents' satisfaction with, 28-31, 42-46; presumption for mother, 2-3

Dating, 129-130; 142-143
Daycare, 112; attitudes toward, 115-116, 120-121; national demand for,

120; problems affording, 113-114; social policy on, 154-155
Dinnerstein, D., 156-158
Discipline, and fathers, 80-82; 84-85, 89, 96-97; and mothers, 76-80, 82-84, 89, 96-97; and joint parents, 90-95, 96-97
Discrimination, in credit, 64-65, 71; in employment, 133-134, 135; in housing, 62-64. See also Stigma
Divorce, effects on children, 4-8, 152; statistics on, 1
Divorced families, compared with intact families, 152-155; cultural images of, 4-5, 108-109

Erikson, E., 16

Family Protection Act, 154
Father absence, effects on children, 4-8; in intact family, 152; limitations of research on, 7, 8
Fathering, attitudes toward, 1-2; future of, 157-158; infants and, 111-112; research on, 8, 10-11
Feminist movement, 1, 157
Friedan, B., 110
Functionalism, 15-16

Galbraith, 73
Gender, social organization of, 1-2, 8-11, 155-158
Gersick, K., 10
Goldstein, Freud, and Solnit, 11-13, 21, 53, 96
Greif, J., 13

Harlow et al., 9
Herzog and Sudia, 5
Hess and Camara, 7
Hetherington et al., 7, 18, 75
Homosexual parents, and custody, 143-144, 155

Housework, and fathers, 101-103, 104-105; and joint parents, 106-108; and mothers, 99-101, 103-104, 108, 110

Income, 55-59; and joint families, 67-68
Intact family, problems of, 152-155
Isaacs, M., 52

James, H., 50, 54
Jens, K., 103
Joint custody, arrangements, 37-38; attitudes toward, 320; children's feelings about, 46-48; closeness between parents and children, 117-119; criticism of, 12, 150; deciding on, 38-41; defined, 3; discipline, 90-97; housework and, 106-108; how time is spent in the two houses, 48; money and, 67-70; parents' satisfaction with, 42-45; problematic joint families, 48-52, 54; pros and cons of, 53, 71-72, 96-97, 150-152; review of literature on, 11-13; two sets of rules in, 91-93

Kelly and Wallerstein, 52. *See also* Wallerstein and Kelly

Lasch, C., 152-153
Loneliness, 123-124, 140, 145-146

Maccoby and Jacklin, 9
Maternal custody, closeness with children and, 116-117; history of, 2-3; pros and cons of, 29, 151
Methodology, 17-19
Misogyny, 156-157
Money. *See* Income
Montalvo, B., 51
Moving, and fathers, 62-63; and joint families, 7-71, and mothers, 63-64, 146
Parsons, T., 1, 6, 16
Paternal custody, closeness with children and, 117; pros and cons of, 28-30, 53, 151

Poster, M., 15
Presuppositions, 14-15; author's, 15-17, 152

Raschke & Raschke, 8
Reeves, M., 139
Relatives, 126-128; and joint parents, 141-142
Religion, 131-132
Remarriage, 130-131, 144
Roman and Haddad, 12-13
Rosenthal and Keshet, 11
Rubin, L., 62
Rutter, M., 7

Salk, L., 26-27, 52
Sample, composition of, 18
Santrock & Warshak, 11
Shelly, P., 2
Shinn, M.B., 5
Sibling relationships, 139
Singles groups, 126, 141
Social security, 65
Spock, B., 1, 120
Stack, C., 13
Stigma, 132-135, 144-145
Study, limitations of, 17; measures and results of, 18-19; purpose of, 13-14; sample, 18
Substitute care, 112-116
Support groups, and children, 135-140; and joint parents, 140-143; and single custody parents, 124-130
Sweden, daycare in, 9; vacations for parents in, 119
Systems theory, 29

Tender Years doctrine, 2, 3
Therapy, 128-129; 142

Visitation, arrangements, 33-35; children's feelings about, 35-37; how visit is spent, 36, 37

Wallerstein and Kelly, 6-7, 18, 52, 152 (*See also* Kelly and Wallerstein)

Weiss, R.S., 3, 8, 12, 17, 123, 147
Working, fathers and, 59-60; joint

parents and, 70-71; mothers and,
60-61
Woolf, V., 73

About the Author

Deborah Anna Luepnitz received the B.A. degree from Kent State University in 1972 and the Ph.D. in clinical psychology from the State University of New York at Buffalo. Dr. Luepnitz is currently on the staff of the Philadelphia Child Guidance Clinic, where she was an intern in 1979. She has published several articles on divorce.